RECLAMATION

A Tale of Blood, Betrayal, and Bioregional Meat

Brad Dingman

Feral Visions Media

Ithaca, New York

Reclamation: A Tale of Blood, Betrayal, & Bioregional Meat

First Published by:
Feral Visions Media
www.feralvisions.org

ISBN: 978-0615674759

Book cover constructed by John Twentyfive
25 Designs © 2012
johntwentyfive@gmail.com

Photographs by JoBeth Dingman

Copy Editing by Scott Barvainis

*Immeasurable gratitude to JoBeth
for your constant support. Now I know why
authors tend to dedicate books to their partners.*

*Also, thank you to Scott Barvainis,
John Twentyfive, and Alicia Beebe for your
contributions to making this project a reality.*

*And special acknowledgement to Alyce Adams,
literary counselor and nurse extraordinaire.
www.kegelqueen.com*

CONTENTS

Prologue. 1
Pilgrimage. 6
1. Crisis. 11
2. Violation. 34
3. Metamorphosis. 58
4. Regression 87
5. Birthright. 118
6. Opportunity. 148
7. Recovery. 175
8. Survival. 212
Epilogue. 241

PROLOGUE

"Early in the new time he had learned the most important thing, the truly vital knowledge that drives all creatures in the forest – food is all. Food was simply everything. All the things in the woods, from insects to fish to bears, were always, always looking for food – it was the great, single driving influence in nature. To eat. All must eat."

Gary Paulsen, *Hatchet*

I'm not known for my patience. Yet, for some perplexing combination of reasons (some of which I don't understand myself), I get up at a godforsaken hour to get out to my spot well before the sun rises over the horizon behind me. I wait with my back against a tree, sometimes catching a snooze, anticipating that moment when the silhouettes that make up these woods just begin to develop a hint of color and texture, and my blaze orange gloves seemingly begin to glow. Speaking of those gloves, or more accurately, the numb fingers within them, I have an unusual case of "Raynaud's Phenomenon." This disorder basically means my circulation sucks and I have a very low tolerance for the cold. I practically overdose on ginkgo tincture these mornings that I head out. It doesn't help much.

Moments before, it was pitch black – and of course that is when the big buck had walked past me just 15 yards away. I couldn't see him well through the darkness, but I know it was him by that cocky strut. I've seen him patrolling these parts, making the rounds, sniffing out the females. In fact, I had my sights on him the day before … literally. Safety switched off. Finger on the trigger. But I let him go because he was about eight inches beyond my comfortable range. Any other self-respecting hunter would have pulled that trigger. Dammit. And there he was the next day, trotting right past me. He had to know I was there. Perhaps knowing it was too dark to shoot, he was simply mocking me. I'm confident he did it on purpose.

I sit and sit and sit and my fingers somehow get even colder, despite being protected in the warmest gloves sold at the sporting goods store.

As the world begins to wake, so do the gray squirrels, making a racket all around me. This woodlot is infested with them. They jump from tree to tree, dig in the leaves, chase each other in circles, concealing any potential sounds of hooves crunching through the leaves. My brain hurts trying to differentiate between the two. Bastards. I find myself despising them, an Aldo-Leopold-Ranger-Rick-wanna-be. I'm a poser. Throughout all of this, I can't help but wonder how many gray squirrels I'd have to kill to equal the poundage of meat from just one average size white-tailed deer.

There is one red squirrel that frequents this corner of the woods. Unlike those obnoxiously pesky gray squirrels – this little guy is my buddy. His hangout is in a half rotted log on the forest floor not far from me. He knows I'm here too. But this one's more prone to just quietly stop by, seeming to say a quick hello with his cute little eyes, before peacefully going about his business. A little deer mouse dives into a pile of sticks not far from my feet while a red-tailed hawk soars overhead.

Despite the serenity these woods offer, I'm getting frustrated. Looking out at this same setting yesterday morning, it was like Mutual of Omaha's Wild Kingdom. Today, however, the deer aren't around. I've found there are basically two types of written literature out there about deer hunting. One genre is written for the macho, trophy hunting crowd. The other romanticizes the whole idea, as if hunting epitomizes communion with the forest. Maybe. But not at this moment. It's cold. My back hurts. I'm hungry and there's not a deer around.

I will never deny that there *is* something magical about drifting in and out of consciousness and having the sense of your prey be the thing that rouses you; the image of bouncing antlers creeping just above the brambles and dead goldenrod, coming closer and closer. I have experienced those kinds of romantic moments before, in both dreams and reality. At times, I drift into fantasies as I'm sitting in the woods, tuned in to the world around me – not really awake or asleep, but somewhere in between.

In one vision, it's hot. So incredibly, refreshingly hot. The kind of sensation that is so rarely felt, that it reminds me that I am truly alive. Spending most days amidst a society of walking corpses – hollow souls, devoid of vitality – the feeling was unfamiliar but exhilarating. This is where the itch had brought me. I hadn't been searching for anything; I had been called to this place by forces greater than my own busy mind. As my sweaty, bare, tingling skin exchanged energy with the exceptional warmth and dryness of the air, I began to feel something unnameable being replenished, something primal. Perhaps a reminder of things I could never articulate because they were buried so deep beneath layers of culturally induced baggage. I am in a sweat lodge and I feel unusually satisfied.

Another dream takes place in a sort of post-apocalyptic world. I am mostly naked, tracking deer through a swamp with a spear in hand – a handcrafted weapon made from a bone tip attached with sinew and pine pitch complete with turkey feather fletching. I'm stalking through cattails. This isn't the type of pursuit that happens once a year according to dates set by a state wildlife agency, it was literally a part of who I had become. Somewhere in the distance, the city was ablaze and we had retreated to the depths of an outlying wilderness. Trailing the deer like a shadow had become a matter of survival for my family.

I've never been a particularly spiritual individual, but the whispers I experienced in both of these scenarios were undeniable. And what they recited to me was a simple message. You need not feel unsure. You need not feel ashamed. You are a welcome participant here.

So, is this what meditation is? Is this some form of spirit guidance?

Beats the shit outta me.

All I know is right now, hunting hurts.

An unrecognizable bird lands in a Norway maple branch above my head. It is backlit against a bright morning sky, making identification difficult. Hopefully, this bird won't rat me out like the squirrels. With my morning deer ambush here being unsuccessful, I figure I might as well do some bird watching. I slowly reach down to lift my binoculars to my eyes. The bird senses my movement and flies off. Birds won't even cut me some slack. The gunshots going off periodically all around me in the distance are not helping my self-esteem either. When I can't take the discomfort anymore, I get up to walk back home.

Is it all worth it? It depends upon when you ask. Now, I'm discouraged, sore, and freezing my ass off.

I'm going home, where I have the comfort of knowing there's a warm bed, and a freezer literally filled with local free-range meat, including some venison.

Regardless, motivated by some mysterious primordial force, I will be out here again tomorrow, doing this same thing, as on countless days before and to come.

PILGRIMAGE

"If the path be beautiful, let us not question where it leads."

Anatole France

I know what you're thinking, and yes, this is *another* book about food. I wouldn't blame you if you put this down right now, got a bowl of ice cream, and put on a movie. Heck, there are hundreds of these things out there. No doubt you yourself have a collection of various food books on your own bookshelf right now – no doubt written by more qualified people than me. But frankly, I just couldn't help it. I love food. I eat it every day. I think about it all the time. I've spent over half my life contemplating food choices and their various ramifications. From going vegan in my teens to bow hunting deer in my thirties – through it all, I've sought a better way than what has been offered to me. I look around. I feel sad and scared. It's painfully obvious that most people still just don't have a semblance of understanding of what we're doing to our bodies and the planet. Because of food.

Granted, I'm not a scientist. I'm not a nutritionist. I'm not a journalist. I'm not even the host of a reality TV show. I'm basically just a gun totin' hunter-gatherer wannabe with a few ideas, a pen, and a laptop. So, despite acing a community college writing course many years ago, I really don't have the faintest idea concerning the proper way to start a book.

However, like the natural world (something I have a bit of an affinity for), I think I'm going to allow this piece to unfold organically. On the surface, the main subject of the book is about food. More specifically, *meat*. But I'm not even so sure that this is as much the *subject* as it is a backdrop to an exploration of who we are as a species, as undeniable participants in our world. Moreover, it is a question of perhaps how we can be so again, in a fuller, more workable way.

And that's why I feel, though this book shares a similar goal to many others out there, that there is more worth saying. I don't think we should stop at the level of advocating for local foods, promoting the paleo diet, or exploring the omnivore's dilemma. This isn't about optimal ratios of fats, carbohydrates, and protein. This isn't about food rules or shopping the perimeter of the grocery store. This is about getting good old fashioned soil and blood on our hands and, by doing so, unearthing something beautiful inside each one of us.

Throughout this book, I reference the workings of non-agricultural societies. Because nearly all of the earth has been consumed by (and assimilated into) one global, agricultural juggernaut, it is easy to view other subsistence strategies, tribalism, etc., as something of the past. Even I fall into this trap as I write. I do intend, before this book comes to an end, to offer the reader a higher sense of importance regarding where we come from, both personally and evolutionarily speaking. However, it is not only our *ancestors* who lived a particular way. We must never forget that there are non-agricultural cultures living in the world today. They are endangered. Their struggles are all too often dismissed. But they are not primitive or backwards or lost in time because they want no part of this. We must not neglect that fact.

I have little doubt that some philosopher or intellectual or even some angry vegan may be able to find holes or inconsistencies within the case I'm about to make. This is not a dissertation or a textbook. This is merely a tale woven from my own personal experience and understanding. What I know is that I am one person, raised within a culture of domination, who is trying to view the world from a completely foreign perspective. As a civilized being, indoctrinated for over three and a half decades with the mythology of our culture, this does not come easy. It's like trying to teach some language of which I have only just begun to scratch the surface myself, but feel compelled to try anyway before it is extinct.

As a fallible human, informed by an ever-evolving (read: *confusing*) body of research concerning our past, I may be bound to get some things wrong. But I know the perspective itself is not. I know, from a very deep place, that civilization – especially industrial civilization – is destructive to the core. There is nothing confusing about that. And I also know that humans are not destined to destroy. I know that somehow, food – as an obvious source of our sustenance, has had a huge role to play in how we got here today *and* how we'll get out.

The fact is, the topic at hand is a multidisciplinary one. A study of the strategies that we employ to acquire food and the high impact consequences of those strategies to our bodies, our spirit, and the land, flirts with many fields. Ecology, biology, nutrition, psychology, history – I can begin examining this topic through any one of these lenses, but it will quickly get tangled with the others. But such is the way of nature. Single issues and linear paths aren't found in the wild, and when humans try to prepackage things in orderly categories, it usually falls short.

That being said, while I usually shy away from categorization, labels and such, I am committed to the viewpoint that has come to be known as bioregionalism. The notion of attempting to recognize, respect, and make choices that enhance the local ecology is simply sane in a world that is anything but. It seems profound, but living in accordance to place is the catalyst to our very humanity. It's built into our genes. Historically, it is all we've known. Yet nonetheless, somewhere very recently along the evolutionary line, we forgot that food comes from a land base. And the more important point is that when we lost touch with the source of our nourishment, we lost touch with the reality of the order of life. There is no doubt we have become lost. But luckily there remain some maps, however tattered and torn, that can guide us back to the land.

So, think about "food" for a minute. Think about the type of stuff that you identify with that term.

This is, after all, just another story about food.

1. CRISIS

"The road to hell is paved with good intentions."

Ancient French proverb

You've heard the message in books, documentaries, newspapers, songs, junk mail and, in this day and age, even from cunning advertisements for your favorite retail products. The earth is a finite shape with finite resources. "Go Green," whatever the hell that means. Buy your way to environmental atonement.

We live in a globalized industrial economy in which most of the human population dwells in cities. And cities, by definition, are not self sustaining settlements. They have exceeded this capability, and thus require the importation of resources from other places. To think about where those places are is something we really don't concern ourselves with. Nor do we often concern ourselves with the quality of life of the inhabitants of those places. Ahh, the price of luxury. We plug our ears, close our eyes and chant like a whiny kindergartener – "I'm not listening. I'm not listening." Block it out. Keep consuming.

Because we're so good at antics like this, it's hard for us modern folks to conceptualize the following scenario. But humor me.

Imagine living upon an island, which precisely like the earth, is another finite shape with finite resources. We'll pretend this island is an isolated piece of land, somewhere thousands of miles away from the closest continental shore. Therefore, importing resources is an impossibility. Now, just because I like eggs and candy, we'll call that piece of land Easter Island. Now, let's make believe that the Polynesians who inhabited this island began engaging in a type of intensive agriculture, and so it necessarily followed that a socio-political hierarchy emerged characterized by sharp stratification. Populations increased. Resources diminished. (Maybe this isn't so hard to imagine after all.)

Let's just say that those in power began ordering the construction of statues as a means of competing for prestige and status. Monuments that, in order to be erected, each had to be dragged from the place of construction by hundreds of people using ropes. Ropes made from tree bark. Being that this island was composed of lush subtropical forest, there were plenty of trees. But now, because we're doing such a good job using our imagination, we'll pretend (for the sake of argument) that things got out of hand.

Let's just say, in order to fuel a growing population and their luxuries, the island is completely deforested. As in, the *whole* forest. No. More. Trees. Once-ler style. As in, widespread ecological collapse. No more statues. No more canoes to go fish. No more wild food. No more bar-ba-loots or swomee-swans. Soil erosion. Decreased crop yields. Starvation. Chaos. Upheaval. A desperate people resorting to eating rats and each other. We'll pretend that the population on this island crashed from 15,000 to barely over 100 people in a relatively short amount of time.

This is a pretty gloomy picture, and even scarier to use as an analogy for this finite planet we call home. It's a good thing this scenario is just imaginary, right?

Right.

What's that?

No, let's not talk about hunting and livestock and all things meat quite yet. I want to talk about the terraforming of Mars.

The first time I heard about terraforming, I had taken my kids to a local museum. The idea is this. Precisely because the earth has finite resources and biologically cannot support an exponentially growing population and our luxuries, we'll just colonize Mars. This is an unsurprisingly real idea to a number of scientists that rely upon an assumption that the environment of Mars can be artificially manipulated to duplicate that of the earth by introducing rock-eating microbes. Some have argued pursuing this is our moral obligation, our destiny as humans. Moreover, after a half of a century of debate concerning human induced environmental damage, it removes that pesky responsibility hanging over our heads to start acting in an ecologically responsible way. If only those Easter Islanders had thought of this!

Terraforming Mars. It is utterly intriguing how horrendously dumb we can continue to be in our immature determination to uphold an unsustainable lifestyle. When we've destroyed the earth to the point that it is uninhabitable, we'll just erect our statues elsewhere. Until of course, we've destroyed that place as well. I'm not even sure what the next planet beyond Mars is.

***

A few pages ago, I asked you to contemplate the types of stuff you consider to be "food." I understand you might not have done so because you subsequently got all wrapped up in my compelling commentary. So at this point, stop reading for a second and contemplate.

Good.

Just as I suspected.

Sorry to break the news to all you carb-loving, dairy eating, insulin laden folks – but pasta, bread, cereal, cheese – these are not the items of subsistence that our animal bodies have evolved to process. To be fair, there is a growing awareness of these issues. Yet even for those of us who should know better, many items we consider food can only be defined as such by the loosest of terms. Cow milk certainly is a wholesome, complete food … for a baby cow. Likewise, you can give your cute little pet bunny a big ole' juicy sirloin steak for dinner. It might be healthy food for, say, a tiger. But exactly what is a rabbit going to do with it? I love Red Hot Blue corn chips, but I don't suspect they are very nourishing.

The somewhat edible items we mostly eat are the inventions of civilized man. Yet, unless you are an anthropologist, it may not immediately occur to you that we are not civilized by nature. In contrast to conventional cultural mythology, our genetic makeup testifies that we are in fact biologically wild animals. Yes, you've heard it before, but believe it. We are mammals shaped by millions of years of evolution and relations with countless other species. We are wild beings, literally enslaved by a process called domestication, a process that started with food production.

It can be argued that all living matter on this planet is nothing more than food for something else. Humans fit into this picture harmoniously since *Homo habilis* walked around grunting 1.5 million years ago, catching insects and small game and in turn being eaten by large cats. But then, around 10,000 short years ago in evolutionary time, something went wrong. *Very* wrong.

Scientist and award winning author, Jared Diamond, has called agriculture the worst mistake in the history of the human race. A growing number of qualified people agree. I'm going to talk a lot about agriculture and its associated social organization called "civilization" in this book. In fact, I'm gonna demonize the hell out of both. But even I find a plethora of likable things about the world we live in. Heavy metal music. Chocolate. Raunchy comedy movies. And, let's not forget chocolate. I'll acknowledge we have a big ole dilemma before us.

But no matter what any of us say to dispute that agriculture is the single most unsatisfactory choice any group of humans have ever made, the ramifications of this subsistence strategy are nonetheless clear. The world is facing a globalized health and environmental crisis that by all indications will cripple the world as we know it. The Neolithic Revolution – the historical origin of our style of agriculture – was, without a doubt, the impetus for this crisis. To discuss improving the global environmental and health conditions without considering agriculture (and thus the converse strategies of hunting/foraging and horticulture – a main point of this book) is akin to treating leprosy with Elmo Band-Aids.

Agriculture itself, as a human-made attempt to overcome ecological laws *for the benefit of a single species*, is a self-imposed disaster in and of itself. However, during the middle of the twentieth century, agriculturalists began modeling food production after a factory model, characterized by sophisticated technology, synthetic chemicals and intensive, high energy inputs. This modern method of growing food has been fittingly labeled "industrial agriculture." Large scale agribusiness corporations now control the majority of the food supply, and so the consequences of agriculture have all been intensified exponentially as the human population increases exponentially.

If one could take on one global environmental issue as the most essential problem to address, Jared

Diamond may just be on the right path. Agriculture, and in modern times *industrial* agriculture, is the root of most all the others – from soil degradation and the destruction of water sources, to overpopulation, global warming, loss of biodiversity, and the ethnocide of indigenous populations. These epidemics could very well spell our demise, and they can all be traced directly back to agriculture.

Wait. Let's backtrack for a moment. Globalized health and environmental crises? Neolithic Revolution? You're hoping I don't start talking about the Natufians! You probably picked this book up ready to read about killing and eating tasty critters. (And they are.) Or maybe you want more fuel to ridicule your neighbor's vegetarian son. ("The pansy.") Or maybe you're a vegan who wants to write me some hate mail. (I probably deserve it.) In a few short pages, you've already been exposed to unsolicited commentary on Martian bacteria and Polynesians. But the anthropological study of hominid subsistence strategies at various subdivisions of the Paleolithic contrasted with early farming communities arising in the Levant due to the Younger Dryas stadial? Huh?

Look around. Our social structure, religions, sciences, art, technology, politics, architecture, industry – and let's not forget a ravaged world – are all possible because humans began settling and domesticating food. Agriculture is an invention that destroyed hunting and foraging cultures around the world, and the land upon which they flourished successfully for hundreds of thousands of years. An invention that has now brought us to the brink of social and environmental collapse. Isn't it worth a *little* exploration on how this all came to be?

But isn't this a book about meat? I don't know. Is it? Have you ever considered that sustenance hunting and livestock raising are subversive acts that, in a multitude of ways, undermine the Eurocentric, destructive, and dominant paradigm that has engulfed *the world*? Maybe it's just me. Well, grill up some pastured pork ribs and sit back on your camo upholstered sofa. (You know, the one under the twelve-point antler mount on the wall.) Let's travel back in time.

***

Anthropologists debate how old our particular species is. But whether that number of years is 50,000 or 300,000 or older, there is little question that for the overwhelming majority of humanity, *Homo sapiens* and our ancestors lived as hunter-gatherers. Humans, like all animals, lived at the mercy of the natural world. This was not out of a sense of nobility as much as an ecological reality that says the following: To consume too much from the environment inevitably means less resources, and thus an eventual decline in population or starvation. And who needs that when there is so much dinner running around?

This is not to say that pre-civilized humans did not manipulate the environment for food. Some assuredly engaged in horticultural practices which involved land management techniques, seed propagation and other forms of promoting favored food sources. But these practices were characterized by a certain simplicity, and did not cross the line to full-fledged cultivation. And they only supplemented a foraging and largely nomadic way of life. Ecological laws that pertain to habitat requirements, population dynamics, carrying capacity, food webs, etc. that biologists currently apply to non-human wildlife were (and are) just as relevant to human life. Generally speaking, this was the way we harmoniously made our living for hundreds of thousands of years of evolution, as all wild animals do. That is, until a few cultures around the world for complicated reasons began experimenting with a process known as domestication.

Domestication is the process by which human control brings about changes in plants or animals that make them more suitable for human use than for a life in the wild. Others more simply describe it as human-driven evolution. By futzing around with domestication, agriculturalists eventually figured out a way to temporarily bypass the aforementioned ecological laws, intervening in the cycle of life in a way that ensures ongoing benefit to civilization.

Though there were plenty of suitable places for food production across the globe in which hunter-gatherers did *not* turn to agriculture until coerced or dominated, where agriculture *did* emerge, certain ecological conditions existed to support domestication.

For example, in certain areas of Southwest Asia, wild grasses such as wheat and barley grew naturally in abundance due to the warm, moist climate that characterized this part of the world at the end of the Pleistocene era. It didn't take long for some smart pre-civilized folks to figure out they could harvest the ripe seeds for consumption throughout the year. However, the climate began to get drier again around 13,000 years ago and these grasses became less abundant. At the time, many of these people who depended on wheat for survival did what most reasonable people would do, they returned to hunting and gathering food as the environment allowed (being they were smart and all). But some *other* smart folks began figuring out how to sow these crops in places they did not naturally occur. This began a newfangled, unexpected relationship between humans and other species.

I suppose that one could say that both foraging and farming have their moments. It's just that the former has the majority of the benefits and the latter has most of the disadvantages. These folks may have been smart, but unfortunately, they weren't psychic. If they had been, I'm certain they would have stayed hunters.

Actually, at a certain point in human history, agriculture – as a way to manipulate the environment into producing more food – was an experiment that seems to have been taking place independently at several locations across the globe. However, in a number of these early civilizations such as the Maya,

Olmec and others, their agricultural systems either collapsed, were abandoned and/or destroyed. Presumably, these cultures figured out oppression wasn't such a great idea after all and acted accordingly. But back in the Middle East along the Euphrates River, a handful of farming villages were becoming the foundations of a civilization that would eventually spread across the planet like an out-of-control wildfire. And unlike those quitters on the other hemisphere, *we* were sticking to it.

The earliest cities archeologists have unearthed, places like Jericho and Catal Huyuk, are also the places where the earliest evidence of environmental degradation, dramatic population growth, and considerable manual labor have been unearthed. These are the real roots of the Neolithic Revolution.

Despite this series of unfortunate events being slapped with the label "revolution" by historians, these people weren't so special. I mean, yeah, we are all special in our own ways, right? But what I mean to imply is that no one can make the case that the inhabitants of this specific geographical location at this specific point in time had a superior or revolutionary vision of the way humans should live. In fact, an agricultural lifestyle is laborious compared to that of hunter-gatherers. With domestication and farming came nutritional disorders, disease, and other consequences that non-civilized humans never faced. The specifics of "why" Neolithic people took to farming is somewhat up for debate. What isn't is that they were opportunists, like you and me, who had a certain and necessary set of environmental conditions that made the domestication of plants and animals possible when times got a little tough. And once farming became the predominant way of acquiring resources, it was awful hard to turn back.

***

Even given the fact that an agricultural life was more harsh and undesirable, the process built upon itself out of necessity, becoming more significant and harder to reverse in a sort of snowball effect. A snowball on crack – that's what agriculture is. The domesticated varieties of these cereal crops tend to yield more edible calories than hunting and gathering. And although high calories is certainly not the same as high nutrient density (quantity over quality), the logical outcome of an increase in calories is nonetheless an increase in human population.

Such a relationship between calories and human population growth is yet another ecological law, one that humans have yet to figure out a way to even temporarily bypass. *An abundance of calories is a stimulus for population growth.* But the clincher is that *population growth is a stimulus to grow more calories.* Specifically, grains grow fast and are high in carbohydrates, which is why they are the staples of these early agricultural settlements and remain so today. But as populations grew in the Fertile Crescent, and the numbers of settlements increased, they had to be supported by increasing the amounts and varieties of domesticated plants such as peas, lentils, chickpeas, and flax. Animals such as goats, and later sheep, were among the first animals to come under the control of human farmers. These increasing human populations also demanded more farming and thus more space. And because the folks in this part of the world happened to have an assortment of easily tamed resources (wheat, barley, sheep, and goats), they were the "haves" that had the power to spread the idea of civilized life. Far and wide, and at all costs.

For these reasons and more, the scale was being tipped in farther and farther regions away from hunting and gathering, and towards large-scale agriculture. To provide an accurate picture of the roots of our beloved culture, I also feel its of the utmost importance to take a look at the spread of agriculture at those geographic boundaries between expanding agricultural territories and that of existing foraging cultures – in other words, those who were in the way. The fact is that the spread of civilization necessitated that these "savages" be assimilated, displaced, or destroyed. And food producers had the populations and increasing technologies to accomplish this goal. More often than not, the diffusion was violent.

Don't simply think colonization, think annihilation.

I suppose it wouldn't be an inaccurate association to think that, almost anywhere in the world, the ground that grows our wheat and beef has been fertilized by the blood of natives. One of the few ways that those who refused to adopt agriculture were able to survive was by escaping to extreme areas that were not conducive to food production or to areas separated by geographical or ecological barriers. This trend, thousands of years old, can be seen today, where the minute percentage of hunter-gatherer cultures currently exist – in the most marginal and harshest of environments.

Though foraging cultures employ a variety of adaptive strategies, I am comfortable making a few generalizations that are important to the rest of the story you hold in your hands. Land-based people are humans, without being slaves to an intensive agricultural system, that live within cultures that are based on reciprocity, kinship, and community. They are largely egalitarian cultures, not because they are necessarily gentle or pure, but because sharp social stratification doesn't work in a tribal structure. They are humans that have an intimate knowledge of local resources, climate patterns, plant and animal species. These are humans with an inherent right to their cultures, and who could offer *us* some integral wisdom about how to live. Yet for thousands of years, hunter-gatherers have been the victims of a bloody blitzkrieg in the name of … you guessed it … *agriculture*.

In summary, hunter-gatherers did not adopt agriculture because it was working so well, because it wasn't (and still doesn't). It spread because of genocide and displacement of native populations. Their land was usurped for our resources, and this process continues today due to market forces and industrial expansion. What started as an isolated experiment by opportunists, only around 10,000 years ago, had the unforeseen consequence of eradicating thousands of cultures and consuming the world in a relatively short amount of time.

"So what?" you're saying. Is it really such a bad thing that agriculture has spread across the entire face of the globe? I mean, humanity expanded across the whole earth long before agriculture. And later, so did Rock 'n Roll. (And everyone knows I like to rock.) Being successful is not synonymous with being evil. Once again, contrary to a popular cultural myth, I uphold that humanity certainly isn't evil. And, despite what some prude bored mothers might think, neither is Rock 'n Roll. (Except the kind of rock that *is* evil, which just makes it *good*.)

The problem with this particular success story is not that humans are evil, it is that the whole notion of agriculture is rooted in a very dangerous idea. Agriculture is inseparable from the fallacies of control and domination. Civilization, and more specifically, Western civilization (the one that has devoured all others) is based upon many assumptions that stem from these fallacies. Beliefs like progress, expansion, property, imperialism – to name a few. This is not an original, or even very controversial, critique of civilization anymore. But I do feel that people forget that food plays a central role in this story. And so do the countless cultures that were, and still are, casualties in Western civilization's cancerous advance across the globe. Every machine needs a propellant. And in the case of agriculture, the blood of indigenous populations and the ecosystems they inhabit are the fuel.

As a subsistence strategy, conventional agriculture can not be sustained. You see, the word "unsustainable," far from being a marketing term invented by corporations jumping on a green bandwagon, has a definite meaning. Unsustainable means *inevitable failure*. If you are an anti-hunter or are otherwise squeamish about taking an animal's life for subsistence, think about that and what it means for your grandchildren. Agricultural systems, as we know them, WILL fail.

Our lifestyle is based upon a very dangerous idea indeed.

***

The ecological blow that has been inflicted by agriculturists is simply immeasurable. From the beginning, as agriculture spread north from the Middle East and into Europe, it met a climate that was conducive to the growth of forests – forests that had to be decimated to make room for growing cereal crops and raising livestock. But when productivity declined as a result of eroded and decimated soils, the slash and burn policy of dealing with those silly inconvenient forests had to be continually repeated. And repeated. And repeated. Never mind the flora and fauna native to an environment. They were enemies that needed to be eradicated, mere casualties of a war with only one side. Native humans, animals and plants were often obliterated, leaving only those that were able to adapt or co-exist with farmers. Agriculture had descended upon all that was wild and was hell bent on raping it all into submission. This process continued, century after century, until the early twentieth century when the stage was set for a whole new, but perfectly unsurprising, variant on an old theme. The Industrial Age was well underway. Farming was going to get a makeover.

If agriculture had ravaged the environment, intensive agriculture was about to ravage the environment intensely.

World War II is often seen as the dividing line between traditional farming and what has come to be known as industrial agriculture. Others place the date later, around 1960. Up until that time, increased yields in food production were a result of simply destroying your neighbors and expanding the amount of arable land under cultivation. But during the middle of the twentieth century, scientists, rather than farmers, began having more of an effect on food production.

They began to apply genetics and chemistry to increase yields. The age of petroleum stimulated more sophisticated technology including tractors and other equipment along with chemical fertilizers. Farm productivity began growing immensely with these machine-intensive methods. The other trend that began was the move towards monocultures, which meant a move away from feeding families and communities, and towards a corporate-owned food industry. We transitioned from small-scale farms to capital-intensive agriculture. The raising of both plants and livestock became more and more mechanized. In summary, this shift from farming to industrial agriculture can be described as the evolution of growing food to growing commodities.

Whole books can be written on any one of a number of topics that exemplify the fact that industrial agriculture is at odds, in every way, with ecological health. Whether it be on how the horrors of livestock factory "farms" contribute to global warming, or soil erosion, topsoil and water sources contaminated with chemicals, overgrazing, loss of biodiversity, ethnocide, etc. – the list of transgressions against the natural world due to agriculture is extensive to say the least. I have concluded that it is too much of a task to effectively summarize how agriculture has produced a global environmental crisis. But, it's also too important not to try.

Human population growth is arguably our number one global environmental issue, because it is the one that impacts most of the others. We've already examined how agriculture fuels population growth. But I really haven't mentioned what happens to the environment when populations begin to rise exponentially. As more and more people are crammed into small places, warfare ensues, ensuring the reduction of safe and available land to farm. Moreover, as populations increase, more resources are needed. Resources that are, in large part, limited. Additionally, impact on the environment simultaneously increases. The earth, with its finite resource base, can simply not support exponential human population growth indefinitely.

The earth's soil is one of the first victims of agriculture. And the more intensively soils are plowed, overgrazed and cultivated, the greater the impact. While environmental problems such as erosion and salinization are ancient problems as old as farming, they are certainly aggravated by industrial agriculture. It was estimated in 1970 that the United States had already lost one-third of its topsoil. And that was over forty years ago. It is also worth noting that only around one-tenth of the planet's land surface is arable for agricultural production. And the little healthy soil that remains is being leached of life and nutrients due to intensive agriculture. Crops extract nutrients from the soil, especially when they are cultivated so aggressively. In most modern forms of farming, these nutrients are not returned to the soil in the form of organic matter. Instead soils are drenched in artificial fertilizers that do not enrich the soil. As a result, soils everywhere are being blown away, compacted, and laden with toxins. In addition, most meat production takes place in factory farms and feedlots, which produce more waste per head than humans. These billions of tons of feces present a huge environmental problem, polluting the soil with drugs, arsenic, copper, ammonia and other chemicals.

Industrial agriculture also requires the wide spread use of chemical pesticides. These pesticides are designed to kill organisms, so their toxicity is not in dispute. It is impossible for these chemicals to discriminate between "pests" and beneficial organisms and so they adversely effect the whole ecosystem. Billions of pounds of these known toxins are spread by agriculturists throughout the environment each year. The breakdown rate of pesticides released in the environment is variable; often resulting in broad and nonspecific consequences. They travel through the environment in a process called bioaccumulation, poisoning throughout the food chain. Not only that, but agriculture of any kind is dependent on pollinators, many of which are insects. It is estimated that pesticides are reducing the honey bee population by two percent each year. This is just one of the many ways in which industrial agriculture bites the hand that feeds it.

Though we tend to act like it, humans are not the only species on the planet. Biodiversity is necessary for environmental stability. Agriculture has historically been spread by imperialism, displacement and force, pushing other non-agricultural cultures to the fringes and leading to their extinction. While this might not technically be called loss of biodiversity, it is certainly a loss of cultural diversity, and the environmental ramifications of this are impossible to measure as we wipe out the people who have the most wisdom concerning sustainable living. Not only are indigenous cultures going extinct directly and indirectly because of agriculture, but it is estimated that deforestation is occurring on a global level at a rate of 150 million acres per year. As complex ecosystems are being turned into to monocrops, the rate of species extinction is astounding. Researchers today are still attempting to figure out the long term effects of these human induced biological extinctions.

What we do know at the least is that agriculture has interrupted biodiversity. Tilling, mowing, changing drainage patterns and agrochemicals are all elements that have had an adverse effect on wildlife populations. But it is habitat loss that plays the biggest role. Birds, which have long been considered indicators of ecological health, have been among the most affected by the intensification of agriculture. And birds, like the bees mentioned above, are also nature's pollinators. It is a fact that agricultural lands are not the primary habitat for most wildlife populations, and the biotic community requires unfragmented and diverse tracts of native habitat. Not only this, but global warming is driving dramatic changes in the ways ecosystems function, including the ability of many species to survive. A loss of a few species can result in large, harmful consequences. It is a serious concern that agriculture as we know it cannot coexist with wildlife.

You may not mind that most large carnivores have been eliminated from your region. You may not personally be concerned with the Northeastern bulrush or the plight of the Indiana bat. But just keep in mind that you rely on the same systems as they do. If world ecosystems collapse, it won't just be species that you've never heard of that will be affected.

***

I hesitate in resorting to threats in an attempt to move people to awaken from a life of illusion. To sit here and preach about the anguish and destruction that our lifestyle is causing certainly isn't my goal. We've all been smothered in guilt trips since we were born into this culture, and I have no desire to perpetuate that. I'm simply articulating a history as I have come to understand it; one we need to acknowledge. The purpose is not so that we can feel trapped, but to point out that we *need not* feel trapped. The mess we live in, and the way of life we were born into, have been inherited without our approval or choice. This book is, in part, about healing by engaging in the world. But we need, first and foremost, to be honest about the nature of our inheritance in order to break our habits.

With agriculture comes susceptibility to infections and disease, a considerable increase in labor and a devastation of the environment and loss of biodiversity regarding which the ramifications are still yet to be fully determined. With agriculture also comes the annihilation of indigenous societies living within its proximity. It brings the formation of cities, militaries to protect them, warfare, and a host of other ills too extensive to list here. Western civilization has permeated the globe to the point of being the most predominant way of life and worldview on Earth. Moreover, there are a myriad of historical examples of societies collapsing because their members did not address their growing ecological problems. This is our legacy. Fast food, endless war, obesity, climate change, mass extinction, brutality, social media – a culture gone mad. Thanks, guys.

So, after all this, why in the heck would anyone stick with agriculture, you ask? Well, why do YOU? Why do *I*? It is rarely questioned whether this subsistence strategy has any alternatives or can even be sustained. But the evidence suggests that the Neolithic Revolution, which began only around 10,000 years ago, was not necessarily a natural or even welcome event. There are historical precedents for cultures refusing to submit to the slavery that we call civilization. Others tried it because it sounded good, but then later abandoned an agricultural lifestyle in favor of hanging out in the woods where all the good food is. Our culture is perhaps the first to have the advantage of learning from the history of of past cultural meltdowns, as well as others that managed to avoid such a fate.

It *can* be done. One just has to get creative … and perhaps a twenty-gauge.

2. VIOLATION

"Our sustenance now comes from misery."

Jonathan Safran Foer, *Eating Animals*

Jonathan Safran Foer found himself dressed in black, sneaking into a turkey farm in the middle of the night. As an American author and grandson of a Holocaust survivor, he was on an honest quest to make sense out of a lot of the complex issues surrounding the food animal business. As a new father, he wanted to clear up some of his own lifelong confusion concerning diet so he could make informed decisions about what to feed his son. He wrote letters to Tyson and other meat companies to try to arrange visits and ask questions about their practices. He heard back from none of them. And so he took matters into his own hands and decided to visit a typical farm … without their permission.

He didn't know that he was entering a turkey farm holding nearly 200,000 birds. Foer writes about the incident, "Everyone has a mental image of a farm … I doubt there's anyone on Earth not involved with farming whose mind would conjure what I'm now looking at." His feet sank into waste as the sound of machines masked the sounds of the clandestine operation. What he eventually found upon entering one of the sheds was tens of thousands of turkey chicks crowded under artificial lights. Dead birds all around. Many of the live ones were deformed, covered in sores and blood.

The sad fact is that this type of "farm" is not the exception. The sadder fact is that turkey farms are among the less inhumane of the various types of animal factories. This is precisely the type of facility where the overwhelming majority of modern meat comes from.

***

What does it mean to be human? Inhuman? Are there certain acts that are simply just *wicked*? Some rituals so foul and vile that they can actually be labeled inhumane? Are there certain crimes against life so reprehensible that any culture, regardless of their differences, would likely banish the perpetrator without thought?

In the first draft of this book, this chapter didn't exist. It didn't seem to fit the vibe I wanted to convey. It didn't fit conveniently. There are many other books that deal with the subject matter. But then, a couple of things occurred to me. First, knowing the truth about how animals are raised in today's modern factory farms is never convenient. In the same manner it wasn't convenient for the world to acknowledge that millions of European Jews were being tortured and murdered by the German state during World War II. The second thing that occurred to me is that, for all the scornful debate between the two camps, conscientious meat eating and veganism have at least one thing in common. They are both alternatives to supporting conventional, industrial meat. Like it or not, many hunters and vegetarians are allies in a front that stands in opposition to modern meat production.

I said in the beginning that this book is, in part, about food. More specifically, meat. And I would be remiss, if not irresponsible, to not use this forum to attempt to educate my six or seven readers about the horrors of factory farming. During the Holocaust, Nazi policies were relatively overt. Everyone knew what was happening, yet turned a blind eye. Conversely, the industrial meat industry of today commits its crimes behind closed and locked doors. These practices take place behind a veil of lies, while an unknowing public feasts daily on the carnage.

I will spend little time defending whether non-human animals feel pain and anxiety. Whether the animals we eat can suffer or not is an absolutely asinine debate and not even worthy of contributing to. As far as I'm concerned, anyone who would actually take the position that only humans have the capacity to feel pain and distress is nothing short of delusional. They are living in such a state of anthropocentric denial that taking the time to engage these types of people is an exercise in futility. I'm going to assume most people reading these words have at least a half a brain and live in the same state of reality. (Then again, maybe not. You are reading a book authored by me after all.) Either way, I'm going to move forward, operating with a knowledge that we can all agree on. Most non-human animals, certainly all the livestock we typically eat, are sentient creatures, much like ourselves.

Because non-human animals, in this case farm animals, have an intrinsic set of interests and needs of their very own, I say they are entitled to a certain set of inalienable rights. I realize, as much as I try to avoid these fuzzy philosophical issues, they are unavoidable in this discussion. Some people thrive on this sort of tedious debate. I am not one of those people. Instead, I am going to attempt to appeal to the intuition of you, the reader, here rather than your analytical mind. I believe that is more than enough to make a convincing argument. Because we know at one time, not long ago, in this country's history, the consideration that women had "rights" was absurd to most people. The notion that African slaves had rights was even more ludicrous. And there have always been philosophers (usually wealthy white guys) with big words making a fancy case to justify these inequalities and exploit others as they see fit. But we regular folks should know better by now.

We know that dolphins and chimpanzees possess and pass on culture. Elephants cry. Mice feel empathy. Whales show appreciation. We've all heard or read true examples of non-human animal emotion. As already mentioned, there can be no doubt that they feel fear and pain, and there are plenty of heartbreaking stories to prove this fact as well. So this brings us to an important point. There are certain freedoms that all sentient creatures are entitled to regardless of arbitrary differences between those creatures. (The freedom to not be eaten does not happen to be one of these.) The fact that there is a percentage of the human population that profits off of the oppression of these freedoms does not justify them, no more than it justifies slavery. In fact, by definition, natural rights are not contingent upon tradition, popular opinion, or a culture's addiction to cheap meat.

So what are some of these rights that I am asserting farm animals are entitled to? You know them just as much as I do. In fact, our country was founded on some of the more obvious ones, as backasswards as that is. *Life, liberty, the pursuit of happiness.* Sound familiar? Total confinement and the infliction of intense suffering do not fall under one of those categories, the last time I checked. That is why there are animal welfare and cruelty laws that apply to some species (however, usually not too strictly when it comes to corporations exploiting them for profit). Yet, all animals, including humans and farm animals, deserve to live out a life free from tyranny. They have a right to associate with others and tend to their offspring as appropriate to their needs. They deserve comfortable cover or facilities to sleep, rest, play, explore, etc. They need access to clean, healthy, and adequate amounts of appropriate food and water sources. Spatial and/or territorial requirements should be met as well as freedom to physically move about this space. The opportunity to interact with elements such as fresh air and sunlight. To not be subjected to torturous acts.

Having addressed some of these rights, I should also point where I differ from the camps that usually are advocating for animal rights. With observation and awareness, I have come to know that out in the natural world, violence is a part of life. In and of itself, it is no more right or wrong than playing or conflict. Absent our judgement, these things just *are*. Occasional stress and other forms of emotional intensity are also just as natural and take place all the time in the wild. Likewise, so does the transformation from life to death, and the distress that sometimes accompanies that transformation. I want to make it clear that I view violence and stress and killing as necessary, and in the proper context, quite beautiful actually. No animal, no human, has a right to be exempt from this process. This is why I can, in good conscience, take a life directly or indirectly, to feed myself or my family.

But violence and pain is not the same as torment. Stress is not synonymous with prolonged suffering. Killing is very different from torture. The severe misery afflicted upon 99 percent of the animals eaten in America alone is a heinous crime against the natural world and it is unacceptable.

Of course I need to address this.

***

When was the last time you saw a deer, and what was it doing? Perhaps grazing or browsing off in a field with a herd or with its offspring by its side under a marvelous setting sun? Okay. When was the last time you saw a pig? Unless you are a small-scale farmer, you probably haven't. But *millions* of pigs are raised and slaughtered every year in the United States alone. Where are they? In windowless hog factories, intentionally hidden from public view, that's where.

And herein lies the heart of the problem. We don't typically see hogs being produced for food for the same reason we don't see timing belts being produced for cars. Because timing belts and ham are produced in manufacturing plants.

The factory. A symbol of the industrial age itself. Machine based manufacturing where uniform products are generated en masse. There is not time or concern for individuality or craftsmanship, as these things reduce the profit margin. As the twentieth century progressed, agriculture was being turned into agribusiness, and it was not long before our desensitized view of life took its toll on livestock. People got addicted to low meat prices in the same way they are addicted to cheap energy prices. Of course, "cheap" is not the correct word at all, because in both of these cases, there is a severe, even if temporarily hidden, cost to be paid by someone or something, somewhere.

Pigs. Intelligent and affectionate. In today's day and age they are raised predominantly in total confinement facilities. These animals spend their entire short life, from birth to death, packed indoors by the thousands, usually without bedding. Breeding sows are kept in a continual state of impregnation and in cramped crates, sometimes tethered or chained to the ground. Their movement is restricted to standing up and lying back down, literally for months, until they are brought to slaughter.

All factory systems are designed to make more money by increasing the output and reducing the cost of input. Animal factories accomplish this by a couple of means that both revolve around intensifying the process. Increasing the output is accomplished by jam-packing the animals into large, metal warehouses – like sardines in a can. Except, unlike the sardines, these animals are still *alive*. In order to crowd them like this, producers have to disregard any need of the animals' that doesn't simply keep them alive until they are of size to slaughter. The envelope is constantly being pushed in this regard as indicated by the large percentage of animals that prematurely die from the consequences of these overcrowded conditions.

The second means to increasing profits is reducing costs. A very small number of employees are required to run one of these intensive operations as all processes are mechanized. At these facilities, automated feeding and slatted floors are increasingly operated by computers. Electronic lights and ventilation fans attempt to artificially recreate a type of day that would speed productivity. Windows and fresh air would only disrupt that process. On some farms, solid and liquid wastes are recycled and added to the animals' feed and water. Other than periodically removing dead bodies, individual care is a thing of the past. Forget monitoring their well being, it's inefficient. So, the friendly, sensitive and wise pig, along with millions from her clan, is reduced to a mere tool of production.

***

The exponential growth of the chicken industry due to mass production is considered a modern success story. For whom, I'm not quite so sure. But before industrial agriculture, it has been said that a chicken for dinner was a rarity. Traditionally, chickens had a niche to be respected on the family farm, and they took many months to grow to full size. And because hens laid eggs as well, they were kept around for a while. Unfortunately for the chicken, mass production changed that.

I'm not sure I need to get into the gory details of the way in which meat birds are confined. The steps are roughly the same as for the hog mentioned above. Take a farmyard animal and figure out how to turn it into a manufacturable product. The cheapest way to do to do this is to pack genetically altered breeds of chickens by the thousands into poorly ventilated, windowless sheds. Here, they are subjected to a mechanized environment that assaults the chicken's very nature so that they can grow faster, until they are violently hauled to slaughter before they reach two months old. And now, thanks to these "innovations," literally billions of chickens can be slaughtered and sold, making quite a lot of cash for a very few large corporations. But though good for profit margins, confinement of animals is problematic. Because animals, no matter how domesticated, still have instincts and needs.

Chickens are social, hierarchical animals that thrive in small flocks. Confined to sheds with thousands of other birds, they get stressed when they cannot act out their social order and this stress manifests itself in the form of unnatural vices such as unusually aggressive pecking and cannibalism. Such unruly behavior costs money of course, and as a result very dim lighting is often used along with a procedure known as debeaking, in an effort to thwart the problems caused by overcrowding. Young chicks routinely have a portion of their beak cut off by a hot blade, often mutilating them in more ways than is obvious. Broiler chickens have been known to panic and pile on top of each other to the point of suffocation.

Layer hens are even worse off. Much worse actually. Most egg laying chickens, nearly 300 million in the U.S. alone, are confined to battery cages. The battery cage system is perhaps one of the most atrocious institutionalized ways in which our culture treats non-human animals, and it exemplifies all that is wrong with factory farming. The confinement of hens takes the form of of being packed, several per cage, to the point that they can barely spread their own wings, let alone fulfill the inalienable rights mentioned above. These cages are stacked, tier upon tier upon tier upon tier upon tier …. Imagine being stuck for over a year in a closet with four other people with a wire floor so your excrement can fall through and pile up beneath you. Above you and below are rows containing thousands of others in the same situation. Almost all hens are debeaked in the painful manner described above. Not only this, male birds born at a hatchery are useless to the industry, so millions of male chicks get disposed of in the cheapest way possible, either by being thrown in a dumpster or ground up. Alive.

We've already mentioned hogs. But we haven't mentioned how they react to the barren, boring, and torturous methods of confinement. Like chickens – like anyone – they tend to go insane. On concrete floors, with crippled legs, they exhibit signs of neurosis. They bite at the bars of their cages. When not crammed in gestation crates, stress due to overcrowding leads to abnormal behavior and aggression. They fight and bite each other's tails. In response to this, the industry responsible for debeaking chicks has come up with a comparable solution for pigs – tail docking. They simply cut off the pigs' tails with pliers.

Turkeys, pigs, chickens …. All of these animals spend their lives breathing in ammonia and other noxious gases. Air in these sheds is polluted with dust and other irritants from animals and their own waste. If it weren't for large ventilation fans, they would in all likelihood suffocate to death. It is common for animals to grow physically deformed or become mutilated from a variety of factors. It goes without saying that these animals, due to intensive confinement and horribly unnatural diets, are highly susceptible to infections and diseases. This is true to the point that these mechanized mega-farms could not exist if these animals' feed was not laced with antibiotics. And still, a surprising number of animals, collateral damage if you will, do not live long enough to even see the slaughterhouse. In fact, I'd say its safe to conclude that the surprisingly high pre-slaughter mortality rates in these facilities provide pretty strong evidence for widespread physical suffering.

***

Farm Sanctuary is one of the leading organizations at the forefront of farm animal protection. They have been exposing the plight of modern farm animals and the secrets of the meat industry for nearly thirty years. They accomplish this through a variety of efforts, including advocacy, education, and political involvement. The organization started as a rescue operation and runs two shelters for farm animals who have been removed from abusive situations. Based in Watkins Glen, New York, they started their first 175-acre animal sanctuary. It's not too far from home actually.

In fact, I once tried to get a job there in my mid-twenties. Cute girls worked there, delicious vegan food was served, and a whole lot of cuddly animals were available for, well, cuddling. Animals that once knew only fear and isolation were now free to roam green pastures under the best of care. I figured it'd be a pretty rewarding job, and besides, I would have earned a ton of scene points. But I didn't make the cut. I suppose my life may have taken a very different direction if I had. As it happens, I now eat animals, and yet still find time to visit Farm Sanctuary with the family every now and then. I view the place through a slightly different lens these days; I can't quite get down with their agenda in its entirety. But there are still occasionally cute girls that work there, the food is still good, and there are more cuddly animals than ever. More importantly, Farm Sanctuary is still engaged in this all too important undertaking that started many years back with the rescue of a young sheep named Hilda.

With relatively small amounts of publicly available information documenting industrialized animal agriculture at the time, the activists who would found Farm Sanctuary decided that in order to be legit, they would need to get firsthand knowledge. And as Jonathan Safran Foer would find out some twenty years later, this was not an easy task. Ask a small-time family farmer to show you around, and you'll assuredly get a proud farmer walking you around the property, talking your ear off until he or she needs to get back to work. I can testify to that. Try to get into a factory farm, on the other hand; chances are you won't get past the barbed wire fence. I can testify to that as well.

They ended up at Lancaster Stockyards in Pennsylvania, which was handling over 300,000 animals a year at the time. Repeated investigations of the stockyard would find significant numbers of dead, dying, or otherwise injured or sick animals randomly left around – either sick from the conditions in which they were raised or hurt at the stockyard during the rough unloading of animals. Apparently, stockyards commonly have what is called a dead pile – an area, as the name suggests, to pile the carcasses of livestock that didn't make it. On one of their visits to Lancaster, they found a sheep lying near the dead pile. Amidst the stench and maggots of rotting carcasses, this young sheep lifted her head and looked at them as they walked by.

Hilda the sheep became the first resident animal at Farm Sanctuary. This type of scenario is so common, the industry has a name for it. These animals, too injured to walk or stand are called "downed animals" or downers. Because of the conditions in which they are raised, these animals suffer from sickness and disease, often to the point of incapacitation. Dairy cows specifically are subjected to such unnatural and intensive milk production, that their bodies are abused to this point regularly. Think on that, all you lacto-ovo vegetarians.

Now that I've gotten that unfortunate little jab out of my system, I have a legitimate question. Have you ever tried to move a 2,000-pound body that is crippled to the point it can't get up? Neither have I. I can't imagine its a pretty scene.

And in fact it's not. These downed animals have to be shocked, dragged, pushed, or poked with chains, tractors and forklifts. There has been video footage of animals being left to die unattended and frozen to the ground. Living, breathing creatures, left to rot in dumpsters because the farmers don't want to deal with them and neither do the stockyards. As if the abuse that brought them to this point was not enough. Hundreds of thousands of animals per year are estimated to be downers. Through the efforts of Farm Sanctuary and other such organizations, the USDA has implemented a policy that states downed cattle cannot be slaughtered for meat. In other words, they can't enter the food chain. The ban, however, doesn't apply to pigs, sheep, goats, etc., which of course, makes absolutely no sense whatsoever. Do you think there are loopholes to find when it comes to reduction of profits? Yup. Do you think its enforceable to any effective degree? Nope.

So, perhaps you're bored with hearing these horror stories. Perhaps you don't even like animals and have little concern for their welfare. But you do like food, don't you? Would you like some bovine spongiform encephalopathy with your burger? Some gangrene with those pork chops? Filet Mignon with hepatitis? Cancer ham?

These practices are simply not acceptable by any sane standards.

Just around the corner from where I live, there is a small family farm that raises heritage breed cattle. These guys would never meet modern production standards. They're too different, too cool. I love looking for them out in the pasture whenever I drive by. I've long had affection for cows. I was barely sixteen when I stopped eating them. I gave up beef before I stopped eating poultry and other flesh. It was actually a couple years before I was to give up milk, cheese, eggs and the rest of any food products derived from animals. I didn't eat beef again until I was thirty-five. That's nearly four years after I reintroduced meat back into my diet. And the only reason I started eating beef then was because I failed to get a deer that year and around the same time, a farmer acquaintance was selling shares of the three pastured beef cattle he had raised. Nineteen years is a long time to disavow eating an animal that the rest of the United States consumes, like, 20 billion pounds of each year.

As a child, I remember annually traveling down across the state to my father's rural hometown to stay with our grandparents for the weekend. I have a few vivid memories from these trips. One was passing the Petrified Creatures Museum and looking through the trees for a glimpse at one of the outdoor dinosaur replicas. The other was my scary grandfather and his chewing tobacco. But the other (and actually relevant) memory was looking forward to being able to walk down the country road to visit the dairy cows. I remember hoping to pet them, their huge towering forms in relation to my small body. The flies. The summer heat and humidity.

I also grew up next to a family dairy cow and sheep farm. The house I was raised in, located in sub-urban Rochester, was in a neighborhood adjacent to the farm's pastures. The town developed around this farm; it remains a bit out of place to this day. There was often the smell of straw and manure in the air. It was a smell that, while other kids in the neighbor-hood complained about, I tended to find pleasant. Occasionally, the cows would get loose and run wild in our little suburban housing complex. Later in life, I distinctly remember my first trip to Farm Sanctuary and the warmth that coursed through my veins at being able to touch, even hug, an animal that was otherwise a staple of the conventional American diet. In modern times, across the world, cattle are even considered sacred in a variety of mainstream reli-gions, most notably in India.

Why this affinity for one genus of farm animal above others? For me, it could be a psychological response to fond childhood memories. It may be a reactionary response to convention. But I now have a different theory.

Cattle are of the same order of mammals that con-sist of several species that humans have historically relied upon for subsistence. Horses, bison, deer, ante-lope … mammals that the human species has depended upon throughout our evolution. Hunting these large mammals and ones like them over millennia honed our senses, and made us a more creative and intelligent species. We owe our very humanity to large mammals. Have you thanked a ruminant lately? And today we can look at cattle, as one broken species looking upon another, and perhaps for a moment remember a time when we were once great together.

But back in reality, that time is long gone. Because today, eighty percent of the beef cattle raised in the United States ultimately belong to four corporations. Tens of millions of cattle. It becomes more challenging to romanticize life on the range considering this. And even harder when you consider that no matter how free they may have lived at one time, they spend the last several months of their lives on industrial feedlots.

See, the industry obviously doesn't like to use terms such as "factory farm." They probably like "concentration camp" even less despite its accuracy. What the meat industry and the government call them is "Concentrated Animal Feeding Operations." Sounds better, right? Either way, virtually all layer hens, meat birds, veal, and hogs are undeniably raised on CAFOs. However, in many cases, beef cattle still spend a short portion of their lives roaming open spaces. That's why the beef industry still uses imagery of cowboys and talks a lot about raising cattle with the best of care and being stewards of the environment. But make no mistake – tens of millions of cattle spend the last three of four months of their lives on factory farms … err … I mean, Concentrated Animal Feeding Operations.

Down on the CAFO, cattle are not animals, they are actually considered "units." By this time, their horns have usually been cut off or cauterized. This is done without anesthetics. The males have been castrated. Without anesthetics. Branded with a hot iron. Without anesthetics. All this so they can be fattened up and overcrowded more easily. Because of mass production. They may not be confined in cages, but how much more enjoyable is it being packed 900 units per acre on dirt lots with no shelter from extreme weather? Dusty. Dirty. Not much fun at all. Imagine the manure?

People like to complain about hospital or cafeteria food and usually with good cause. But that nasty mac and cheese is gourmet fare compared to what cattle get to eat on CAFOs. The point of feedlots, by definition, is to provide a place for cattle to be "finished." If you don't know what "finished" means, it means to be fed a diet that will transform a steer into more money in its last stretch of life. Talk about crappy food. It doesn't much matter that a diet of corn and other grains fed to a ruminant gives it acid indigestion, bloat, inflammation, and ulceration of the liver, and assists the evolution of dangerous strains of bacteria that kill little kids. Or that unhealthy animals mean nutritionally inferior meat that can cause a host of health problems for the people who eat it. Nah, that doesn't matter. Fat, grain-fed cattle means fat wallets in the pockets of ranchers and businessmen.

**

What doom and gloom ridden chapter, such as the one you are reading, would be complete without a tale of environmental degradation so bloodcurdling that it serves to scare the bejesus out of us all? Facts and figures and stories of ecological deterioration that ambush you until you go out and hug a tree or at least buy a solar powered lawn light? If the last chapter wasn't enough to intimidate you into action, well, I've got more. So, without further ado....

Modern livestock production is a bane upon the natural world if there ever was one.

I suppose I need to explain a little more.

We can start with a generalization. Factory farming and the grains utilized to feed factory farmed animals cause mass deforestation, species extinction, overgrazing, soil erosion, desertification, and water pollution.

It has been estimated that eighty-five percent of all U.S. agricultural land is used to feed livestock. That is an incredibly vast amount of once healthy ecosystems. Forests, wetlands, and prairie turned into endless fields of corn and soy. Hundreds of millions of acres of once stable, dynamic, and diverse wildlands turned into chemical pesticide saturated monocrops growing on chemical fertilizer saturated soil. An immense amount of the planet's biomass is being turned into factory-farmed meat. This loss of biodiversity and resource depletion is not only unsustainable, it could very well prove to be *catastrophically* unsustainable.

But that is not the only environmental issue related to factory farming. An equally disturbing issue is that no matter how much agribusiness attempts to mechanize the processes of birth and death and all those inconvenient processes that affect profit margins in between, there are certain things they just can't control. Animals still poop.

Few rational people dispute global climate change anymore. While the massacre of billions of farm animals is the most obvious result of factory farming, there is an environmental toll that threatens the lives of countless *other* creatures. Casualties of industrial livestock production are not just cows and chickens, but also include the the Hawaiian akikiki, elkhorn coral, bull trout, Canadian lynx, bog turtles, and flatwoods salamanders. And the reason these species and many others are on the verge of total annihilation is, in part, because livestock waste produces emissions. And a lot of them.

So what do hydrogen sulfide, methane, ammonia, and nitrous oxide have in common besides being compounds that neither you nor I understand? Come on, I know you hated chemistry class as much as me. But we don't have to be chemists to agree that these are potentially poisonous compounds. And what they have in common is that they are emitted in the form of gases from animal manure and cause atmospheric pollution.

What's important here is that while carbon dioxide gets all the climate change press, it isn't the only culprit. Methane's contribution to global warming is not to be underestimated. It is twenty-five times more effective at trapping heat than carbon dioxide, and one of the main contributors to global methane emissions is livestock. Nitrous oxide is next in line on the list of most destructive greenhouse gases. And again, due to intensive livestock operations, concentrations of nitrous oxide in the atmosphere is on the rise. Just as the evidence for global warming can no longer be dismissed, neither can the fact that modern animal agricultural methods have a huge role in the planet's changing climate.

And what does one do with billions of tons of animal waste anyway? More and more often, the waste generated by factory farms is stored in giant lagoons. "Cesspools" would be a more appropriate term, but the industry doesn't like *that* one either. Manure and urine is collected in pits underneath the animal confinement sheds and then periodically flushed to the lagoon where bacteria supposedly break down the waste. The poisonous concoction of shit, pesticides, antibiotics and other toxins is then often mechanically sprayed on fields. Yum. Of course, these systems fail time and time again. Overflow. Runoff. Widespread river pollution and coastal water deadzones. Fish for dinner, anyone?

As traditional farming practices have been replaced by industrial style operations, the potential for the healthy incorporation of livestock in an ecologically sound food system has been all but stifled under the solid waste produced by modern confinement practices. Today, what is common is the obliteration of healthy soil, water, and air within the orbit of such factory farms.

And on top of that – now my dinner has been ruined, I'm depressed and absolutely sick of writing this chapter, and almost want to go vegan again. Almost, but not quite.

***

Once upon a time, in the not too distant past, we worshipped the animals we ate. We bowed to their exuberance and felt deep gratitude in our hearts that they had chosen to give their lives to us. We honored them in our rituals, dances, and ceremonies. We painted their sophisticated and fluid figures on cave walls. We emulated them and attempted to capture a bit of their strength, courage and ferocity by carving hybrid creatures out of ivory or limestone. We recognized and gave our respect to the rights of the Buffalo People and the Horse People. We walked with the wolves and mammoths as if they were our kin.

Today, we confine them. We abuse them until they are crippled and broken. We medicate them in order for them to barely survive their short lives – lives spent in misery, suffering in their own filth. We mechanically slaughter them in droves as if they were inanimate parts on an assembly line, wrap them in styrofoam and cellophane, and sell them for $2.99 a pound. And then we wonder why our society is so sick.

3. METAMORPHOSIS

"You can never solve a problem with the same kind of thinking that created the problem in the first place."

Albert Einstein

Now that the onslaught of depressing information from the first couple chapters seems to be over, for the meantime, we can move on to other things. Perhaps it's time for a story. Heck, everyone loves a good story. Before we get more into this notion of what a bioregional approach to acquiring meat looks like, you might be wondering about how I got here after having abstained from eating animals for so long. What I've come to find out is that my story is not unique. For more and more people, the transition from veganism to conscientious omnivory and even hunting is happening in a very logical way.

One year, a national animal rights group made posters for the annual "Great American Meat-out." The poster depicted a caricature of a hairy caveman "savage" gnawing on a raw meaty bone next to a clean-cut white man in a suit eating a salad with utensils. The poster proclaimed something along the lines of "Are you still living in the stone ages?" I was vegan at the time.

Not only derogatory on several levels, the image of ancient man as malnourished, dirty and plagued by disease is completely divorced from reality. By the end of this book, I intend to make the case that those so-called "cavemen" were actually affluent and successful in a way that we have a difficult time comprehending. The aforementioned images, along with terms such as "prehistoric" and "primitive," serve an important historical function to civilization – to barbarize a way of life that is a viable alternative to our own, thereby justifying its elimination. I was a bit shocked to see my peers, while claiming to fight inequalities by organizing a "meat-out," engage in a campaign driven by such ignorance. But I digress. This is not a book about derogatory terms, it is about food.

No matter how far our species attempts to deviate from the natural order from which we are created, we can not get away from certain things. Like every other creature in the animal kingdom, the fact is that we need to eat in order to survive. And like all terrestrial organisms, from the tiniest microorganism to the largest mammal, it is through this link that we are completely and intimately connected to the soil and the sun's energy, and thus the whole of life.

As discussed in the last chapter, in modern times, and in the most nonsensical of ways, the life forms that we literally rely upon to survive have been industrialized and oppressed in ways that are almost unspeakable to anyone who cares about the natural world. Add to this fact, as the food we consume has been increasingly processed and altered beyond the point of recognition, the human race has gotten sicker and weaker. These combined and inseparable phenomena have prompted a great many lost and confused people to search for answers about what our natural diet is supposed to look like. It is no wonder why diet fads change like the wind and on any given bookshelf labeled "nutrition," one finds a plethora of diametrically opposing viewpoints about what that means.

And what does this have to do with this amateur author talking all this jive about subsistence strategies? Quite a lot. For most of my life, I have cared in some capacity about health, nutrition, and the state of the world. It turns out that the answers to these questions are not nearly as complicated as so many would have us believe. But, at times, these types of concerns have defined me.

It seems inevitable, after an estimated ten thousand years of dietary degeneration, some feel an answer has emerged to this crisis. Some feel it is in the organic or local food movements, or in the fight against genetically modified food. More and more are trying raw diets, while others turn to the doctrine of the Weston A. Price Foundation. Some are self-proclaimed fruitarians. Fruitarianism? *I thought this was a book about meat!* Believe me, the *second* someone comes up with The 30 Day Sausage Diet, I am on it like flies on roadkill. Regardless, increasing numbers of people feel the answer actually lies in veganism. On the surface, it makes a degree of sense.

If you haven't heard, veganism is a diet in which one abstains from all animal products – meat, dairy, eggs, honey and the like. I feel I am kinda qualified to discuss veganism because I was vegan for nearly thirteen years. That's almost half my life. And much to the chagrin of the proud carnivores reading this, I can speak almost endlessly about the benefits I have personally received from following such a lifestyle. Is it time for another history lesson? So exciting! This time, it's about a self-proclaimed militant animal rights activist.

***

I would have liked to start this chapter off with something extraordinary. For example, I got into animal rights early on when I rescued a baby puppy from being beaten by an armed gang of dog fighters and it became my childhood best friend. Or that my father worked in a slaughterhouse and brought me for Take Your Child to Work Day where I was peer pressured by a group of teasing, heartless men into rendering a steer unconscious with a captive bolt pistol, and as I did the deed, I saw a single tear roll from its eye, changing my life forever. Or that my babysitter was a founder of the Animal Liberation Front and took me on nighttime covert missions to free monkeys from the labs of vivisectors while my parents dined and assumed we were home playing Twister. Nope. Bummer.

The boring truth of the matter is that I was brought up in a loving home by parents with good intentions. Picture the white Cape Cod style home in a suburban development. We lacked the white picket fence, but had the rest. Minivan, soccer, you name it. In retrospect, I was nonetheless an angry young man by my mid-teens. I was picked on enough for being different in one way or another until the point that I hated school. I hated society. I had few friends. But I found comfort in angry music. Punk, metal, hardcore. Many of these bands espoused a message of nonconformity and fury at the established order. Some were quite political. Some even spoke, or screamed as the case may be, in defense of the environment. These types of bands gave a voice to the underdogs, and that voice resonated with me on an intimate level.

The fact is, there's a whole generation of very pissed off kids out there. It's perfectly understandable, but very scary. You've heard this story many times, though I didn't turn to drugs or shooting up my school. Instead I channeled that anger towards activism. I was lucky in a certain sense to find a social network I was comfortable in. I was vegetarian at sixteen. Vegan by eighteen. I wore, among other things, a T-shirt with a hunter sighted in crosshairs. I had a tattoo of a cow being slaughtered with the words "Never Again," and another that said "Vegan Power" (Needless to say, they've both been covered up by much cooler tattoos).

The mid-nineties was a unique time in the history of activism in the defense of animals. The youth were seizing the reins, without asking, from an older and passive generation of animal advocates. We saw them as ineffective and inconsistent. Counterrevolutionaries. At the time I was becoming a core member of the movement in the area, there was already a sizable animal rights organization in town. I distinctively remember the last meeting I attended before finding my own path with my own peers. Someone had vandalized a local fur store and the preexisting local group in question was discussing at length how they needed to reply to the police and media in order to distance themselves from the action at all costs. They were to publicly disavow any such activity. They intended on fully cooperating with the cops and apologizing to the store owner. *Apologizing*? I walked out of that meeting and founded my own animal rights group in town not long after.

One with a goddamn backbone.

I was organizing and participating in protests, both locally and out of town. Our group was one chapter of a predominantly student-run coalition based in Syracuse. Due to our strategic use of direct action, we became such an effective force that the Federal Bureau of Investigation initiated a campaign, for all intents and purposes, to harass activists and neutralize the activities of the organization.

It was a fun time really. We'd hang out, get arrested, yell at women in fur coats, have vegan potlucks. You haven't lived until you've been hogtied and dragged through a mall department store. The movement fulfilled a needed sense of belonging; it gave a sense of power to those of us who were in many ways rejected otherwise. And despite a dose of self-righteousness, our intentions were in the right place. There was no insincerity whatsoever in my striving towards empathy and compassion. After all, there is no shortage of unnecessary pain and death in this world, and I truly felt that I had stumbled across the answer.

Like the pioneers in the struggles against racism, classism, and sexism of the past, we were paving the path that would hopefully become the next great social justice movement. And we saw ourselves on the side of the abolitionists and other notorious revolutionaries of the past. We weren't asking for animal rights. We were demanding animal *liberation*. I was out to defy any tradition that taught that humans were superior to all other species, including but not limited to, the consumption of meat, eggs, and milk. These were, without exception, mere acts of oppression. I believed that it was impossible for humankind to ever be released from that which ails us, so long as we continued to enslave innocent animals. But in the end, it was an immature analysis of some very critical issues.

Even today, I can still speculate with a fair degree of confidence about the benefits veganism has to the animals and the environment. Despite the fact that I've personally killed, gutted, and subsequently eaten a number of animals at this point, believe it or not, I would still defend veganism to a degree. At least as it compares to the destructive traditional American diet. In fact, it has been said that vegetarians were the original food activists. Since early on in the evolution of agriculture there have been those associations of people, guided by a code of ethics, who have abstained from eating animals. The Essenes, Buddhists, Hindus – all guided by a higher purpose to reject violence in favor of compassion. And still yet others striving towards better health than the deal offered by agriculture. It was these ideals that inspired me.

Becoming vegetarian, and later vegan, directly led to a higher ecological consciousness. It led me to intrinsically value the processes of life. It made me aware, in a very substantial way, that something was wrong with the imagined hierarchy we conveniently place ourselves at the top of. It allowed me to begin making a connection to other aspects of creation. It taught me that not only are we humans animals, but that non-human animals are sentient creatures worthy of respect. It has taught me a great deal about nutrition and cooking, and given me a much greater appreciation of what we put into our mouths. Veganism has contributed to an immeasurable increase in the value I personally place on the processes of life. It eventually made me question the validity of the structure of civilization itself.

So I have to give credit where credit is due. The misconception still permeates the majority of the population's perception that the animal products they consume are raised on small-scale family farms where they graze and carry out their natural instincts in idyllic conditions, in harmony with the environment. When a shopper picks up a pack of chicken wings, they see dinner. They do not see the remains of crippled animals that were crowded in a filthy warehouse with thousands of others, barely able to move, never seeing sunlight. Let's be clear: Old McDonald is a lying bastard. Agribusiness goes out of its way to cover up the hideous reality of intensive animal agriculture that is the common practice today. And the fact is, it is vegetarians and vegans who are exposing these otherwise hidden practices, not meat eaters – even the principled ones. So to them, I raise a glass of almond milk in toast to their efforts.

***

So where does this leave us if we don't want to support this mechanized wholesale torture of animals? It left me with veganism. Logical, right? It is an obvious solution, at least on the surface. But see, there is one more lesson that I learned from being vegan for all those years. I now uphold, regardless of dietary fads that change with the wind, we would do well to be more appreciative and intellectually honest in this life. It would serve us to not pick and choose only those arguments that support some pre-conceived ethic or opinion. Much to the dismay of the vegan community, I thankfully learned something from veganism that belongs in an altogether different paragraph than the previous few.

What veganism has taught me … is that veganism is not the answer.

***

The "butterfly effect" is a theory that states if a butterfly flaps its delicate little wings, it could potentially set off a chain of atmospheric conditions that could alter the path of a tornado in another part of the world. The point being, how can someone determine the complex web of events that stimulate a given change? The question I often get, maybe the one that is crossing your mind as you read this, is when, where, and how did this dramatic shift in dietary philosophy possibly take place? As I mentioned, veganism defined me for quite a while. News of my breach of the vegan code was often met with shock, treated as a bona fide fall from grace. I had some serious explaining to do for simply adding free-range eggs and fish into my diet. But hunting and raising livestock? Nah, it can't be true. And now *a book* telling people they should go out and kill animals? I don't presume a flapping, pretty little insect is going to suffice for an explanation. Well, it makes perfect sense to me. I sit here, snacking on bison jerky, trying to figure out how to articulate it in a way that makes sense to others. And unfortunately, I simply can't think of a cut and dried answer.

I distinctly remember picking up Euell Gibbon's *Stalking the Wild Asparagus* for the first time. It was an old, ragged copy left on the table at a local hip vegetarian restaurant of all places. While the book remains today a practical bible to the foraging counterculture, there are several chapters towards the end about eating meat. The book bluntly discusses the prejudices we all harbor against certain food choices, specifically those from the animal kingdom. Frog legs, crayfish, turtles, porcupine, muskrat … armadillo sausage? It's all nutrients, and the author of the most well known book dealing with wild edible plants was condoning it all. It was unconventional enough, despite all my vegan inclinations, to find utterly intriguing.

In fact, being born into a culture that has so obviously lost its way has led me to be often intrigued with that which is unconventional. If modern Americans find an otherwise sensible and healthy behavior as outlandish, it may be a good sign there's something to it. Like, eating whole monkeys. Being the nerd that I am, I like being exposed to information concerning the practices of indigenous cultures, ancestral knowledge, and the like. I remember reading such a book revolving around the Senoi of Malaysia – an aboriginal people who reportedly did not eat much meat. However, as a treat they would cook a whole monkey carcass – organs, bones, hair and all – over a campfire. Monkey fingers were considered a delicacy.

If that's not cool enough, David Attenborough is the shit. Or, should I say, Sir David Frederick Attenborough. (Cue Bette Midler singing "Wind Beneath My Wings.") Mr. Attenborough (as if you don't know) is a famous naturalist who, among a list of other achievements, has created a whole series of programs for BBC related to ecology. One particular documentary about mammals shows footage of a hunt being carried out by the San, one of the few remaining tribal people living in the Kalahari Desert. Without exaggeration, the first time I saw it, it left me in a state of awe. It was not because of watching such an alleged cruel and barbaric ritual. Quite the contrary, my astonishment arose because it was so incredibly beautiful. Watching the hunter and prey engage in this rhythmic relationship where both parties were in total, unexplainable tune with each other. The event was an eight-hour hunt, and the entire time both parties were living, breathing and sharing each other's pain.

While none of the preceding examples convinced me to sell my vegan cookbooks and use the profit to go out and get a bacon double cheeseburger, they were beginning to have an impact on my opinions about meat. Contemplating that BBC footage of the persistence hunt, I cannot think of any activity in modern civilization that even comes close to this type of intimacy with nature. (Since I wrote this paragraph, I have watched the film *The Great Dance: A Hunter's Story,* a full length documentary about the San and their hunting methods and stories. My recommendation is to put down this book *right now* and figure out a way to watch this.)

It was this sort of knowledge that was slowly and insidiously eating away at what I had held for so long to be absolute truth. And so, for many of my vegan years, I did not abstain from animal products because I thought that killing animals for food was necessarily morally wrong. I had many examples that proved otherwise. I remained vegan because it was easier than any alternative to the cruelties of factory farming than I could come up with. The mounting evidence, and subsequent questioning, was not enough to make my dietary convictions bend. No, not yet. Stubbornness is an area of expertise of mine, and I was too invested in my own identity. And moreover, I was still addicted to the feeling of standing upon that moral high ground.

***

But what are morals and ethics? I can tell you one thing, they are not absolutes. For example: cannibalism, abortion, sexual promiscuity … these things absolutely work for a surprising amount of cultures, and absolutely do not for others. What promotes harmony within one society may be a sign of degeneration in another. While ethics are important, they are subjective. They are the means by which humans makes sense out of what could superficially be seen as chaos, and sometimes they shift and change. I don't presume that many land-based cultures assume they have the authority to dictate their own moral conduct onto their neighboring tribe any more than a pride of lions forces another to hunt like they do. This imperialist mentality is a product of agriculture, and in turn, I was a product of this mindset. It can be argued that there are some universal morals, such as an obligation to care for one's children or prohibitions against incest, but discussing these is beyond the scope of this book. My point is that a universal *dietary* code of conduct is about as far away from such an example as one can get. Which basically means my perceived moral high ground was more akin to smoke and mirrors, and I was having trouble seeing the trick myself. But over the years, some moral dilemmas inherent to my vegan philosophy were beginning to surface and becoming harder to justify or ignore.

Western morals aside, the domestication and suffering of animals in today's industrial model of farming is a plight that I have never been able to ignore. Add to this the environmental ramifications to the soil, air, and water by intensive animal agriculture, and one capable of empathy could (hopefully) admit these practices can not be conducive to a healthy society. But eventually, one has to question whether the seemingly obvious answer of veganism is truly the best way to bring an end to these violations against the natural world. What one does with that question once it has arisen is another topic. But the question itself is nonetheless a valid one that, at some point, I began to contemplate more and more.

I speak from personal experience when I share the opinion that conventional veganism ignores the ecological interactions between human and non-human species. Humans are above the savage habits of carnivorous animals, right? Humans have the capability to reason, which separates us from the rest of nature, right? We have dominion over the earth's creatures and so are obligated to safeguard them, right? *Wrong.* As a vegan, I mentally removed humans from their place in the cycle of life, however unintentionally. The irony of course, is that this is precisely what agriculturists do, and look where doing that has that gotten us. Unlike what philosophies such as veganism suggest, the killing of animals is not a black and white ethical issue that can be dealt with as such.

Eventually and gradually I was coming to what is perhaps the biggest flaw in this line of "ethical" reasoning which is the assertion that eating a plant-based diet results in the end the killing of animals. An assertion that I stuck with despite years of tending to backyard vegetable gardens and noticing the countless chopped worms and slain spiders. And the question that logically followed, at least for me, was that if my very small-scale backyard gardening involved the death of animals, then can I imagine how many deaths necessarily occur on the gigantic mega-farms of today? How many groundhogs, rabbits, and rodents are slaughtered by the blades of tillers and plows? And this isn't even counting pesticide use. One could (and I did) take this argument even further by pointing out how many fossil fuels are used in the production of vegetables, between gas powered machinery and synthetic chemicals. Polar bears are heading towards extinction due to loss of habitat from global warming. How many raccoons are run over by trucks transporting vegan food across the country? No matter how I sliced it, even the most organic vegetable farm cannot escape killing animals.

Even while eschewing all animal products, it seemed fair to me to compare a hunter who kills a deer on his property (one animal dead), to the vegan buying processed food from California (countless animals dead). I began admiring the hunter a little more than the vegan.

And then, of course there is the issue of the conventional and most common way of growing the food that we civilized folk like to eat (including vegans). It is an argument that, over the years, has become more relevant in discussions about sustainable food systems. Monoculture is a crime against the animals and environment if there ever was one. The endless acres of soybeans and corn required to make most processed vegan food necessarily means a loss of biodiversity, and an increased vulnerability to ecological collapse due to disease, pests, and environmental degradation. Displace and destroy the lives of countless native animals in place of miles and miles (and miles) of corn and soy? Deplete the soil and its inhabitants of all its worth? I had to ask myself … are these practices *vegan*?

As a vegan, I was more in tune with certain realities and less in tune with others. One such example of a reality I was not attuned to was the fact that it is undeniable that organic plant agriculture is in part dependent upon animal agriculture for fertilizer. If there was no manure and other animal by-products to be recycled for organic fertilizer, there would be an exponential increase in the use of synthetic fertilizers in agriculture. (Compost alone could never meet these requirements.) By and large, our vegan veget-ables exist because the soil was either doused in an abundance of harmful petrochemicals, or fertilized with the organic material generated from the back end of domesticated livestock. The environmental impact of a total reliance on agrochemicals would be unimaginable. And coinciding with this, the demand for genetically modified crops would increase as well. Are these the paths I wanted to pursue to end the killing of animals?

My plan here is not to demonize vegetarian philo-sophies. However, these are some of the dirty little secrets that most strict vegans either haven't thought about or don't want to think about. At least I know that *I* didn't want to think about it, because these arguments were a threat to much of what I presumed and advocated for years as truth. I was a voice of the voiceless after all. I had compassion and justice on my side.

But the facts remain, and me being me, with my striving towards consistency, I couldn't deny them forever. I had known that for a millennium before us, humans ate animals. I was seeing that the laws that govern all life on the planet cannot be categorized as "wrong" by our invented subjective cultural values.

***

Let's take a math quiz. Take one vegan warrior. Add one vegan woman. Enter some evolutionary biology of a different sort. And what do you get? That's right … a vegan baby! Surprise!

During the first couple of years of my first son's life, I was no longer an active participant in the animal rights movement. I had lost the desire to focus so much energy on a single-issue cause, one strand of a much deeper problem. Not only that, but I had been secretly questioning the doctrine of the animal rights community for some time and didn't want to be a part of it. But through it all, I remained vegan. I could not bring myself to sever the ties that grew from my diet. And having a vegan child only reinforced my sense of commitment to the oppressed animals of the world. But then, something else happened. She got pregnant again.

When my wife was pregnant with our second child, she was still nursing our first. She continued a vegan diet as she had for years without much question. It came to a point where she was literally feeling drained regardless of how much, or how nutritiously, she ate. She was doing all the right things, eating a variety of organic plant-based foods, and taking a high quality prenatal supplement at the time as well. She began having a gut feeling that she was missing something in her diet. That something we could not account for considering the quality and quantity of her diet. Discontinuing breast-feeding was not an option at the time. After all, nursing is a truly natural behavior that every mammal exhibits. Perhaps needless to say, this situation combined with my own struggles with fatigue lead to countless conversations and introspection about veganism, diet, and nutrition.

The truth that I did not want to acknowledge for well over a decade is that I physically was not well. I was overweight and unfit. I was exhausted nearly all the time. I couldn't relate to the … ahem … libido that other men seemed to exhibit. And what fun is that? It wasn't. I was sick and had been for years. Not the kind of sick where I was vomiting or fevered or hospitalized. But debilitated nonetheless. I had put up with it for years, secretly wondering how others who ate much more unhealthily than myself seemed to feel so … *normal*. The last thing I was going to do was acknowledge the possibility that veganism was the culprit. But having my partner, bun in the oven, feeling anything other than exuberance, was not acceptable. She was at least brave enough to admit it and that encouraged me to finally embrace reality. This uncompromising commitment to a lifestyle that, in all honesty, I had known for years to fall short had to come to an end.

The first flesh that I ate in almost fifteen years was a sustainably harvested tuna sandwich. Made with vegan mayonnaise of course. Perhaps the most emotional meal I had ever had in my life.

***

Let us all give up. Walk right past the nutrition section at the bookstore, without stopping, on your way to the hunting and firearms section. We consume more diet books, magazines, and blogs than we do food. There are many misdirected, if not falsified, arguments given to support this diet or that. And while there certainly is money to be made, there is no "perfect" diet. Never has been. Never will be. I know the arguments, because I have used them all myself. Ailing people desperate for a program on what they should eat probably don't want to read peer reviewed anthropology journals. So, I'll sum it up: humans are biologically omnivorous. And plenty of opportunities exist out there with scales and fur and feathers.

The fact is that while the benefits of veganism are plentiful, it is simply not the only answer to the very complex question at hand. Humans are a diverse and versatile species. We evolved in a multitude of geographic locations and varying climates. Our ability to adapt and consume a variety of types of food is part of what has made us so successful (if that's how one chooses to describe what we have become). In fact, veganism is far from the most natural or healthful answer. For those of us who honestly care about food issues, animals, and the environment, we must step off the moral pedestals we have fooled ourselves into thinking we stand upon. It is in the interest of our health, in our future, that we embrace our biological make-up and put nourishment back in the proper context of evolution.

While much research has shown the benefits of a plant-based diet, it is undeniable that certain people, if not many people, do not thrive on a strict vegetarian diet. I don't doubt there are quite a few vegans out there that could kick my scrawny ass. But many others have complained of symptoms such as lack of energy, depression, weakness, eating disorders, etc., not to mention more severe nutritional deficiencies such as anemia.

Nutrition aside, the fact is, when humans lived in most harmony with their environment before the dawn of totalitarian agriculture, there were as many diets as there were cultures. As mentioned already, they were hunters, foragers, horticulturists, and always opportunists. They ate according to what their bioregion produced in terms of edible material, which varied from locality to locality. Before the dawn of agriculture, these bioregional approaches to diet were universal and more important than the nuts and bolts of nutritional science, as it should be so today.

Other than a dependency on place, Paleolithic diets really had only a couple of attributes in common. One was that they didn't have the hands of self-proclaimed nutritional experts in their pockets. And another characteristic that was shared between thousands of cultures covering thousands of miles over thousands of years, is that *none* of them were vegan.

***

In the Star Wars prequel trilogy, Anakin Skywalker's descent to the dark side of the Force, although gradual, was not completed until he severed the arm of Jedi master Mace Windu. After Windu is killed, it is then that Palpatine accepts Anakin as his official apprentice. In the tradition of the archetypal fall from grace, Anakin fulfills the inevitable transmutation into Darth Vader in a desperate attempt to save his pregnant wife. The movies suck, but it's a great story.

There I was, just like that jerk Anakin, after years of questioning and eventually doubting what I had come to know as noble and right, at a crossroads. Me and Anakin, with our pregnant, ailing wives and our intensifying moral dilemmas. Ugh. His destiny was sealed when he severed the hand of the Master of the Jedi Order. Mine was actualized with the severing of the head of a chicken.

My vegan edge was broken by that fateful bite of tuna flesh. Subsequently, I officially incorporated wild fish and pastured eggs into my diet, still eschewing dairy products while maintaining an overwhelmingly plant based diet. But I had refused to eat any domesticated and slaughtered animals until I had butchered one with my own hand. This was my self-imposed prerequisite to eating meat. I believed then, as I do now, that one has no right to ingest another animal's body unless they would be able to, at the very least, view the deed with their own eyes. Preferably, while partaking in some intimate manner in the process of the taking of a life.

There was a common catch phrase back in the day: "If slaughterhouses had glass walls, the whole world would be vegan." It is my experience that most privileged people live in a state of intentional ignorance, closing their eyes and ears to any reality that would threaten their lifestyle. It is because of this fact that gross violations can be committed against the land, indigenous peoples, and animals without opposition. It seems to be an unspoken agreement between the public and the institutions that uphold civilizations. We'll turn our heads if you lock your doors and carry out your filthy acts in secrecy. My objection to this insanity was not going to change whether I was an herbivore or a carnivore.

***

Live poultry, enter stage right. Weapon yielding suburban kid, enter stage left.

***

Catching chickens is not easy. Especially when it's winter and you're freezing and unprepared. Sure now, several years later, having kept chickens in my backyard, I am much more used to it. My children can even manage some success scooping them up. But back then, the closest thing I had experienced to nabbing up a live chicken was opening the refrigerated case at the grocery store to capture one of those elusive packages of Tofurky. I was nervous. This was all new to me. And chickens, despite being on the stupid side, are annoyingly agile in their own chicken-y way. Especially to a suburban vegan veteran.

But Chuck, my slaughter coach, was not going to have me escape any part of the process. He himself did not grow up a farmer. His was a product of Corporate America. A good portion of his life, he had played the game – owning businesses, making money. He got out in favor of organic farming. And in the process, he had to learn these skills himself. Because of that experience, he wasn't going to let me off easily. That's my theory anyway. Maybe he was just a sadist that liked to stand there watching me frustratingly chase after chickens flapping in every which direction. I no longer remember how many birds I slaughtered on that cold day out at the farm. It was less than ten, but I had lost track. The whole process was so physically and mentally stimulating that the details were blurred a bit. However, with Chuck's prodding, I had made sure I did it all. I gathered them up, one by one. I took their lives. I pulled out their feathers. I scooped out their warm entrails with my own bare hands.

Upon sharing this story, it follows that I have been asked more than once how it felt to kill those chickens after being a strict vegetarian for so long. For most of them, I chopped their heads off with an axe. The first couple I watched flail around, blood spewing everywhere like a gratuitous horror movie. This method was a bit disorderly for lack of a better word. With blood stained snow and poultry feathers everywhere, I then decided to hang them after making the crucial cut. It was no doubt exhilarating. I distinctively remember feeling a child-like sense of pride in myself. The gratification of learning something new.

But my sense is these answers aren't satisfying for people. They wanted to know if I felt sad. The truth of the matter is that, while slaughtering is not something that I could do all day, I did not feel an ounce of sorrow. If anything, I felt guilt for *not* feeling sorrow. I did feel empathy, which is very different than sorrow. Above all else, I would say that the process felt very *natural*. But I do recognize the shortcomings of that poor adjective. Instead, I think the more accurate way to summarize my feelings about the ordeal is that it made me feel alive.

**

It was nearly a decade ago now when I was put in touch with an author of a book I had once read. The book was a sort of memoir of a tramp. It was about living a figurative life on the run, full of train hopping, petty theft, and hitchhiking tales. The author swore off working and was committed to evading the monotony of the American dream. The book was humorous and inspirational and appealed to the rebel within me.

It turned out, this person welcomed our being put in touch with each other with a degree of excitement. Not only did he know who I was which was surprising enough, but as it happens, words I had written many years ago had actually been partially responsible for him taking up a vegan diet and getting into activism. Little ole me. I was impressed with his character, and I think he was with mine. We interacted through e-mail off and on for many months and were both stimulated by the conversation. It was like a modern *Letters to a Young Poet* between two aging discontented vegans. I never met him face to face; he was a transient and didn't like to stay put too long. But oddly enough, I did consider him a friend. At some point, I lost contact with him.

I had no idea what had happened until the FBI showed up at my door one spring afternoon. This wasn't the first time I had been visited by federal agents. But it had been quite a while. My usual response was to ask if I had been charged with anything, and if not, close the door. Before I had the chance, it was explained that my phone number had been found stored in the cell phone of a man who was just arrested. I closed the door and put two and two together. Shortly after, I received a letter from a friend of his explaining things.

My mysterious pen pal, whom I had known by a different name, had just been arrested in California after successfully eluding federal authorities for seven years. I met him while he was a wanted man. He had been indicted on charges relating to the liberation of thousands of mink and fox from multiple fur farms and the destruction of breeding records at each farm. At his sentencing, he addressed the court and said his only regret was not attacking more fur farms and publicly told the fur farmers sitting in the courtroom that raiding their property was the most rewarding experience of his life. This dude was badass and I loved it.

We had written a couple times while he was in prison and I donated to his legal support fund, but ultimately I had ended whatever few and far between interaction we had left. Not because I didn't value him. The truth is, I was embarrassed. This guy, a peer roughly my own age, was sitting in prison for acting on his beliefs. His defiance in the face of animal abuse was amazing to me. While he stayed true through it all, I could not maintain a philosophical loyalty to animal rights and veganism. While he had literally been successfully thwarting federal agents for years, I had been questioning everything I had thought to be true. The outspoken radical vegan kid that had, in some manner, helped influence this hero, had sold out. I had bought a house, had kids, gotten married and starting eating animal flesh. How could I explain this to him?

In a similar vein, I was recently watching a documentary about Paul Watson, the founder of the Sea Shepherd Conservation Society, and a man I greatly admire. The Sea Shepherds are an interventionist marine conservation organization who are known for tactics that others may deem … we'll say … intense. Lo and behold, there I see on the screen before me, two ex-acquaintances of mine on board the Sea Shepherd vessel in the Southern Ocean, helping to attack the Japanese whaling fleet. I haven't talked to these guys in years, but apparently, at least as of the time of filming this documentary, they're still vegan, and still involved in high profile direct action against animal abusers.

I don't know what any of these guys would think of me now, or what any of my old peers would think of me. I have a genuine appreciation for those taking a physical and philosophical stance against institutional animal cruelty. Heck, I still take great pleasure in hearing of mink operations destroyed and watching illegal whaling ships get rammed. Furthermore, I would still gladly stand by their side in opposition to the horrors of modern day factory farming. However, in my experience, I'm not sure many vegans would want to stand by me.

***

Regardless, I am much more confident in my journey at this point in my life. I abhor the industrial meat industry. I recognize the endless health problems wrought by a conventionally raised meat-based diet in this society. I consider factory farming an abomination – a felony against the order of life, a waste of resources, and a tremendous threat to the environment. But I uphold that veganism, in the end, caused *me* harm in more ways than one. What I have come to see after years and years of contemplating these issues is that we don't have to choose between the American meat-based diet and veganism. Both of these diets are extremist and out of balance with our very humanity, thereby inevitably impairing our potential for wellness. Besides, if I never started eating meat, I would have never discovered chipotle cocoa crisp bacon, and that would have been a damn shame.

As much as it may sound, I am not now a loyal disciple of Weston Price, or a committed proponent of the Paleo Diet. I feel a great respect for the logic and principles behind these ideologies, yet they are still atomistic programs promoted by marketers that are subject to the same conditions that all fad diets are. I no longer define myself by a diet. Nonetheless, our ancestral roots cannot be ignored if we ever want to know health and freedom. We are primates. We are apes. We are humans, which is fundamentally different than the civilized beings most people consider themselves to be. We are, without a doubt, primal creatures, sculpted by millions of years of coexistence with the natural world. We must acknowledge these realities in order to make informed choices. And so therefore, my choice is to now approach food issues holistically, not only recognizing, but *embracing* the aforementioned realities. Like it or not, that includes consuming animals.

4. REGRESSION

"The aboriginal peoples and poets were right all along."

Randall L. Eaton, *The Sacred Hunt*

I was not going to be content eating only animals raised in captivity. I was not going to accept purchasing packaged cuts of meat from Walmart. I wasn't going to make this choice without getting my hands dirty, nor should anyone. Within a century, the industrial food complex has usurped the healthy raising of animals from the people. They have taken animals from free ranging out of doors and confined them behind closed doors. In addition, hunting has been in decline for decades. In the process, we have lost skills, wisdom, and vitality. When we left the raising and killing of animals for subsistence to the globalized food industry, real savagery and brutality were given the green light.

The time is ripe to take it back into our own hands, creating land and community-based food economies. While I think there is something to that phrase "by any means necessary," I have done the protest thing and have personally found it ineffective in relation to the energy spent. To me, what is effective is simply reclaiming this vision and the associated skills as our own. To the novice foodie, there is perhaps an irony to the fact that by re-learning to kill, we are actually liberating animals from being sentenced to enslavement. In that process, we are also liberating ourselves.

There is a roadmap to this path of liberation, as old as humanity itself. Some farmers and gardeners have found it. A few anarchists. A city planner here or there. Many indigenous cultures never lost it. I believe (and I think billions of factory farmed animals would agree with me) that the time is overdue we modern meat eaters took a look at this age old concept that has a new name. It's a word in the title of this book, but we've barely mentioned it. So, what exactly is *bioregionalism*?

According to my interpretation, it is a perspective. A perspective diametrically opposed to the civilized perspective. It's not environmentalism. It's not green politics or socialism. Its not preservation. These are flawed, sometimes very flawed, ideologies. However, everyone and every thing undisputedly lives within a bioregion. And that arrangement seems to have worked for quite some time.

***

There was a time when we acted as if our environment was our source of nourishment. Silly ancient superstitions. I hate to belabor the point – no, actually I don't, it is too important – but humans and the rest of the community of life *are not incompatible*. And until about 10,000 years ago, that crazy thought would not even have occurred to anyone. We lived as one species among many, which all relied upon each other and the land. That is the key. We were reliant upon *the land*, and so our activities enriched that land. Not in some abstract, romantic sense. But in a very substantial and meaningful way.

Food is an essential component of any culture's economy. The modern field of economics implies that it is natural for businesses, households, and individuals to maximize their benefits at all costs. The tragedy of the commons and all that jazz. But it's important to note that an economic system does not have to entail continual growth and negative impacts on the environment. Money is obviously not inherent to an economic system either. In fact, an economic system based on growth and monetary wealth is, quite simply, anti-life. There are alternatives to a capital-based global economic system that views nature as nothing more than a pile of resources to exploit for the goal of gaining profit. Our present culture, as a whole, is just not humble and honest enough to attempt to understand other social systems (such as that of land-based cultures) that might undermine our inflated sense of self-importance.

I know it is heresy to suggest that ecosystems have value beyond that which can be provided to us consumers. Our system is fueled by the viewpoint that nature is good because it is usable for humans. It's obvious that the industrial juggernaut doesn't give a shit who or what it annihilates on its path. But even the most altruistic of us concern ourselves with losing the aesthetic value of nature and then falsely believe we should leave it alone. Could it be possible to have a functional economy if we believed nature is us and we are the land and all of it has an inalienable right to thrive together?

Humans are not slaves or tools. Trees are not obstacles in the way of a future feedlot. Pigs have feelings. *We belong here.*

Heresy indeed.

Luckily, I don't have to be the one putting forth and proving the idea that a sustainable economy based on a reciprocal relationship with the rest of the community of life is possible. I have history on my side. Land-based cultures and their economies do not revolve around infinite growth, nor the idea that nature is something to fence off from humans and preserve. These are relatively new, and dangerous, concepts in human history. If our ancestors had believed in this nonsense like we do, the human species would have never made it to the Holocene epoch, let alone the twenty-first century.

At one time in human history (and still in a few places left in the world), economies – in terms of how a society acquires its subsistence – were based upon the plant, animal, and mineral components of the ecosystem in which that group dwelt. Renewable components. Living components. No oil from Saudi Arabia. No mangoes from Peru. No beef from New Zealand. No timber from the Amazon. The economy was based on what was available and what could be sustained. If biodiversity decreased or the ecology changed to an unfruitful point, they moved or got creative. Again, this occurred not because they were noble savages, but because they were not stupid or blind.

This is not to say that tribal societies never traded beyond their land base. Many certainly did. But they did not rely on the importation of resources like our cities are condemned to do. They relied upon the land upon which they walked, along side a community of other inhabitants permitted to do the same. In other words, they were not removed from reality, like nearly seven billion other people I know. These were holistic economies where the whole mattered more than the sum of its parts. They were egalitarian economies in a way that those of our day and age can barely comprehend. In short, these economies were based upon relative equilibrium and stability – not growth.

Land-based people have their needs met. They are not bombarded with depraved advertisements in every direction they turn, and so "wants" take on an altogether different meaning than in our culture. Where appetites are satisfied, there is little yearning for material items, and addiction to "more" is rare. In an environment of plentitude, where life is abundant, these conditions equal economic sustainability. If it was true that human nature dictates we act only in our own economic self-interest, there wouldn't be example after example of cultures that do otherwise.

It's true. Really. Humans *aren't* just consumers. Even today, there are actual people out there in forests of South America, the subarctic barrens of North America, and the deserts of Australia and

Africa that provide for each other as an automatic, unquestioned element of simply being alive. Even despite being pushed to the most marginal of environments, their economies are sustainable. No one goes hungry.

There exists a few very valid and fundamental questions that one must ask in the face of these facts. Why is it that our global culture has such a colossal problem with the production and distribution of goods and services, when we simply did not have such a problem for the overwhelming majority of our existence? Why does it seem we are constantly on the verge of economic collapse while some cultures live with cradle to grave security? Why is it that when we exhaust local resources, we feel we have a right to pillage and get those resources from someone, somewhere else. And what makes us think this conquest in the name of economic growth can continue indefinitely?

The answer is frustratingly simple. Hunter-gatherers and other land-based cultures have economies and cosmologies based around a bioregion, while we do not.

A bioregion is basically an encompassing ecosystem defined by geography, flora, fauna, soil types, climate, etc.. When such a non-civilized culture cannot import their every desire from elsewhere, there is an evolution of what has been termed Traditional Ecological Knowledge or TEK. TEK is as integral to sustainable economies as money is to ours. And in land-based cultures, TEK is universal. There is a need for an intimate relationship to the land – the collective botanical, zoological, and geographical knowledge of a local culture is the key to survival. This traditional ethnobotanical and ethnozoological knowledge usually far surpasses our own understandings of how the world works and allows land-based cultures to manipulate the environment for resources in regenerative ways. Bioregionalism.

When considering how to acquire a specific resource in a healthy and sustainable manner, it benefits us to look at the common traits in the economies and cosmologies among people who live in a proven workable way. In cultures that work, the inhabited land is seen as sacred, certainly more than simply an economic resource to be drained. In a local economy, draining the land means collapse. Because of this fact, there is an understanding that all organisms that inhabit the same bioregion are inextricably connected and there are ecological limits. In the United States and increasingly around the world, we live in a hyper-individualized society devoted to this notion of growth at all costs. Yet, this is far from a natural state of affairs. Humans are social animals and are evolutionarily designed to work and live cooperatively to acquire their subsistence, but not at the expense of the larger ecological community.

Because of this, land-based people have achieved *genuine* affluence. They have a rich and meaningful existence, documented over and over again by anthropologists. They may squabble. Heck, they might even eat each other or scalp someone or two. I don't have illusions of Utopia here. But the fact is, non-agricultural cultures do not dominate. They do not subdue. They do not eradicate. Their religions and economies aren't built upon a foundation of fear and conquest. There are very fuzzy lines, if at all, between work, play, and socialization. Economic production isn't miserable or on the verge of collapse without artificial interference by the Federal Reserve System.

Such is the case, not because they are better, but because they operate *bioregionally*.

To understand the point better, we can compare such a bioregional approach to a culture with a different approach to reality. Know any? Civilized people are colonizers who think our knowledge is superior to that of the savages we evolved from. We have Bibles, manifest destiny, the World Wide Web, and we are advanced dammit. Our primary function in a global economy amounts to an insidious form of captivity. It is we who have mortgages, credit card bills, major appliances, Internet addiction, property taxes, and Zoloft. Even the more financially well-off in our culture live a life of poverty of the soul. It is we civilized folk who have to slave at jobs we despise all week for an increasing number of hours, to put dinner on the table and iPods in the hands of our babies.

***

So, you've got it now? Those native folks are *environmentalists*, just like you and me and Monsanto. So, we're set. If we just join the World Wildlife Fund, they'll use our money to fight the good fight and protect nature. We just gotta "go green" and our problems are solved. We have to support green businesses like ExxonMobil and Dow Chemical, who are now apparently committed to environmental responsibility. Even PlayStation 3 doesn't even come with a paper manual. It's all about saving the earth.

I'm not so sure about that though. More blasphemy is about to follow.

This is what I tend to think. Eastern screech owls are not environmentalists. Redback salamanders are not environmentalists. Shagbark hickories are not environmentalists. Black swallowtails are not environmentalists. And land-based humans are not environmentalists. All of these are simply examples of the environment *itself*. Maybe the answer doesn't lie in conventional environmentalism as we've come to know it.

***

You see, let me explain. I declare that I am not an environmentalist. The globalization of the environment, no matter how well intentioned, signifies how far we have strayed from bioregionalism, our connection to a land base. To "think globally" is actually the problem. A global perspective of the environment is so overwhelmingly beyond our comprehension that it is frankly unattainable. After all, only a few individuals out of billions have physically seen the planet Earth as a globe. Regardless of this fact, how many environmental organizations and corporations alike use the image of the earth as a way to identify and market themselves? We have people and organizations and products all over the world that are "earth-friendly," whatever that means. The last time I checked, the surface area of the earth was, like, 315,000,000 square miles.

When we, even the self-proclaimed environmentalists among us, cling to this global vision, we necessarily detach ourselves from it, because the world is seen as something *outside* of us. We thus de-localize environmental issues. This perspective leads us to see the earth as not something we belong to, but as something that belongs to us. Has our collective swollen ego lead us to actually believe that the planet needs *our* protection? It is precisely this notion of our relationship to the natural world that has lead to most of humanity's perceived alienation from the environment, and has lead to the very environmental degradation that we now face.

Hunter-gatherers and other local place-based people gain their knowledge of the environment from participation *within* it. The concept of being "within" is hugely important and very much in contrast with the western perception of the environment as a globe. The globe is a solid image outside of us upon which we stand and work, and can never be otherwise. A land-based environment can be perceived of from within. People with a bioregional vision directly engage with the environment, living and making their living from within it. This is the same perception of the environment that the bear, salmon, and deer have as they make their way through the environment. The salmon have no notion of saving the earth. They just do what they've done for millions of years and the fact that they are still here testifies to the fact that it works. Humans would do well to learn this lesson.

Modern people, with their global vision of environmental issues, tend to gain that knowledge in a general and detached way. Our view of the natural world is largely intellectual and gained from books or other media. I am writing a book behind a computer screen. You are reading a printed page. We engage in passive activities such as these over and over. Lather, rinse and repeat and we think we're pretty well educated. One can learn about plants from a plant physiology textbook in which half the words are too difficult to pronounce and the equations are too difficult to make any sense of. Or, one can learn about plants from feeling them, ingesting them, listening to them. Hunter-gatherers, horticulturists, and other local-based people and animals gain their environmental education from experience, which is a much richer form of knowledge. It is immediate and intimate. In many ways, these concepts of how we come to understand our environmental relations mirror my own path.

For many years, I personally had what I would now consider a very modern, urban, conventional interest in environmental issues. My knowledge about the environment was very generalized and theoretical. The environment, as I perceived it, was something beyond my own situation. Recycling, global warming, and animal agriculture were issues that I cared about, however abstract. By the time I began formally studying wildlife conservation and natural history in college as an adult student, I had been a vegan and self-proclaimed environmentalist for years. Yet, I honestly did not know the difference between an oak and a maple leaf. My knowledge and perception of the environment was very superficial. At school, I read Aldo Leopold. I began studying local ecosystems and wildlife management. Rather than becoming broader, my environmental knowledge started to become more narrow and localized. Because of this, a radical reformation of my views took place without an intention of doing so. Thanks Aldo.

The most dramatic shift in my environmental knowledge took place in subsequent years. It is then that I began a nature journal documenting phenological changes, identifying plants, etc. I also dabbled in wilderness skills and wild edibles, and began hunting. I became much more conscious of the natural world, by an increased intimate participation in local ecosystems. I learned so much more about my environment with those types of activities than any of my time in school studying the environment through books and computers behind desks and screens.

My very personal experience, only briefly summarized here, has left me with the very strong opinion that people become knowledgeable about the environment by immersing themselves within it. Every living thing, including us, already has some degree of knowledge or relationship with the natural world. The type of knowledge a person has will be dependent on how they relate to their environment. If one spends time at the office, on Facebook, or watching TV in a sanitized plastic 70-degree environment year round, that is what their knowledge will be. If one is standing barefoot in the rain, harvesting herbs for tea, they are embedded within the environment and their perspective will be quite different.

In other words, in order to gain any meaningful relationship with the natural world, one has to become intimate with their local land base by actively and directly participating in the elements of their bioregion. Becoming attuned to their own situation, perceptions and land leads to a real knowledge of the environment. This sounds like the beginnings of TEK. Beyond that, environmental knowledge can only be generalized. We can study global environmental issues, get a PhD in Environmental Science, be fluent in the technical fields of chemistry, biology, etc. Perhaps there is even a place for these disciplines in solving our current environmental predicament. However, as long as we distance ourselves and humanity physically, mentally, and spiritually from the local community of life, all of our knowledge will only continue to add to the modern environmental crisis. I run the risk of offending people by stating this – but robotic, spectator environmentalists are not what we need right now. What we *do* desperately need are people who play, observe, experiment, track, gather, hunt and dream in the natural world.

The philosophy of bioregionalism suggests – as I do, as indigenous people do, as non-humans do – that the environment is not elsewhere. It does not lie outside of humanity or culture. I believe that those that perceive the earth as an "other" will necessarily partake in actions and make a living in a way that in the short run, may cause disruptions to the earth's systems, but in the long run will also be destructive for the people in question, no matter how green. I fail to see how a culture can be sustainable as long as environmental knowledge is gained by seeing the earth as something separate or below us.

Perhaps anthropologists have more to offer us about our modern predicaments than environmentalists. After all, environmentalism has largely failed in protecting local resources and environments. What makes people think environmentalism will succeed in protecting global resources and environments? If we are discussing issues pertaining to living a lifestyle and sustaining ourselves in a way that can be maintained for a long and continuous period of time, we won't find the answer in what is hip. We won't find the answers from multinational, neocolonial conservation organizations who sell out indigenous people across the globe rather than risk offending their ecologically bankrupt corporate donors. It was after all John Muir, the founder of the Sierra Club, who set the stage for modern environmentalism by arguing that Native Americans were filthy and depraved and that wilderness should be cleared of all human inhabitants.

No. Sustainability can not be bought and sold and is not open to different interpretations based on what is environmentally trendy at the time. It is immature, if not irresponsible, to believe that humans should leave nature alone. The whole concept of even being *able* to leave nature alone testifies to the absurdity of our culture. The only people who ever truly lived sustainably did the *opposite* of leaving nature alone. They were immersed in the environment as are all organisms and enriched it through their daily activities. But these same people, the very cultures we should be emulating if we care about ecological issues, have been the victims of thousands of years of widespread genocide. Atrocities committed by the same folks that brought us modern environmentalism.

Lately, I've been noticing more frequently people claiming the earth as being sacred, and it's starting to annoy me a bit. Not that it isn't true. But so is Jupiter, all of Neptune's moons, and the Andromeda galaxy. Sacred or not, I can't perceive these things, so who cares? What I can begin to try to perceive and understand and thus care about is *this* place. I can smell the soil here. I can hear the roosters. I see the pines, hawthorn and dogwoods growing in the fields. I follow the deer trails and taste the autumn olive berries and blackberries. This is my environment, my source of life, not some blue and green ball I saw on a photograph.

My partner helped me come to this realization years ago before we were married, but living with each other in the city. We were out in our small backyard on a summer day and as memory recalls, I was complaining about living in the city and that I did not have enough time or opportunity in the woods to feel engaged with the natural world. She pointed to all the little plants all around us, the clover, the sorrel, the ground ivy – probably 50 species of plants in that small yard alone that we didn't know – and said, "why not start here?"

We ought to return to a human scale conception of the environment. The earth is the stream in our backyard, the wind blowing snow on our face and the rock growing moss. Our species evolved integrated with these elements and the animals as well. To return some attention to this wholeness – we never left after all – is what living in an ecologically responsible way means to me. Bioregionalism states, "why not start here?"

This is why I embrace bioregionalism, because I value simplicity. Because small-scale is not only beautiful, it is practical, and it's all we ever can truly know. Large scale is synonymous with complexity and an inability to be successfully managed – be it societies, governments, economies, or environmental organizations. Big is vulnerable and vulnerable is not sustainable.

Bioregionalism, although obviously a term coined in modern times, is a primordial concept. It is an inherent component to my interpretation of this concept that we attempt to re-indigenize our minds and communities. We need to reacquaint ourselves with the local, like our ancestors before us. Like the Clovis cultures of North America. Like Turkana Boy, Peking Man, or Lucy. Like the Cro-Magnon hunters. Like the Awa of Brazil or the Pygmies of central Africa or the Jarawa of India struggling for survival today.

When something is in line with millions of years of evolution, *then*, I can get down with that.

***

The "politics of place." That is what bioregionalism has been called. Local production for local consumption. Good enough for me I suppose. All that I know is that each of us lives in a unique ecological and cultural area. And such an area can never be adequately defined by arbitrary political boundaries. In fact, it cannot be defined by anyone other than the inhabitants who are (or more commonly, once *were*) rooted there, or have a history of living in that place while simultaneously enriching it. Because our cultural forefathers pretty much obliterated those that held this vital knowledge, one continent after another, bioregions are often hard to define. Bioregionalism is likewise hard to define. But nonetheless, this movement is growing as people begin to see, as conditions worsen around them, that civilization is destined to fail as is its counterpart, globalism. People are beginning to remember that humans once thrived because of our intimate understanding of place.

Though I was born in the 1970's, sometimes I have sincerely wished I was of an age where I could have experienced firsthand the growth of awareness that arose from the counterculture of the decade or so before I was born. The music, the free love, the rejection of materialism and the first rebellion against all that is the American dream. It would have been groovy, but I was born 25 years too late. Actually, no. I probably would have developed an even an angrier disposition if I would have had to deal with all the other nonsense that came with that period. Either way, thankfully, we did get MC5, and Bob Dylan, and a new term called bioregionalism that would spark some far out conversations.

Bioregionalism evolved out of the San Francisco counterculture of that time. It is unknown who originally coined the term, however it makes perfect sense for describing a territory defined by its living components. Either way, the contemporary vision of bioregionalism began being propagated through an organization called Planet Drum, formed in 1973. By the late 1970's, other organizations in California began adopting this vision. As of today, there are perhaps hundreds of organizations and many more individuals across the world who identify with this movement. Ironically, even global environmental organizations like the Sierra Club have tried to hop on the bandwagon.

Kirkpatrick Sale, author of *Dwellers in the Land* and many other pieces on politics, technology, and the environment, describes four basic natural processes that arise from adopting a bioregional perspective. Knowing the land, learning the lore, developing the potential, and liberating the self. Although I might have used "community" in addition to "self" liberation, I can think of no better simple definition. Thanks Kirkpatrick.

Unlike what the dominant cultural mythology leads us to believe, there are as many ways to live as there are bioregions. So, perhaps it is needless to say, bioregionalism looks very different in the Cayuga Basin than it does in Cascadia. Yet, there are a couple of basic tenets to a contemporary bioregional paradigm that stand diametrically opposed to all we know. They are as inherent to the bioregional perspective as colonialism is to the civilized perspective.

The first tenet is scale. As in *small* scale. Why does environmentalism so often fail? Because the fact is that we are not wired to act in ways that are responsible for those beyond our land base, let alone on the other side of the world. People tend not to act in an ethical manner when they are not directly connected to the problem. To expect the billions of our culture to voluntarily change and live in some abstractly defined environmentally friendly way is simply never going to happen. Never. I don't expect or even *want* anyone reading this book to become an environmental saint. I'll leave enlightenment, salvation and such to your religions. What I would like to make tenable for people to understand is that if your community works towards self-reliance at the regional level – within ecologically defined boundaries – you don't have to worry about these moral dilemmas because the land itself will tell you how to live within your means. By the default of the fact of living on an evolutionary appropriate scale, many of the problems that characterize our society will simply cease to exist.

The second tenet lies within what Kirkpatrick Sale calls learning the lore of your place. Look around at where you are, out a window if need be. That land, in all likelihood, has a rich history of traditions and folk knowledge underneath the lawn and asphalt. That knowledge may likely be rejected by the industrial-scientific interpretation of the world. But look where that interpretation has gotten our species. Bioregionalism suggests that we shouldn't so quickly dismiss the lore of our land. It suggests that the people who lived in this place may have known a thing or two about how to live with it. After all, they *listened* to the land. There is a traditional wisdom about this place, about your place, and bioregionalism rightfully respects it for its inherent value unto itself, as well as for what it offers us today.

The difference as I perceive it between bioregionalism and other catchy environmental philosophies is not *only* its alignment with 99 percent of our evolutionary history. It's not just the identified link between local communities and human satisfaction. It's not just that small scale solves so many of our issues. But it's also the fact that such a perspective can be applied to all arenas of our lives. From economics and politics, to where we source materials and where we live, to the cultivation of native food plants, and yes, even where we get our meat from. Delicious.

Some of those in recent decades who have been associated with bioregional thinkers and causes have taken a position defending a reduction of meat consumption, even advocating vegetarianism. Well, I'm here to change all that. I'm gonna fight for my right to hot dogs blanketed with pulled pork, and wave my bioregionalism banner while doing it.

***

One of the most obvious, and coincidentally most effective, ways to apply bioregionalism is to food. The acquisition and consumption of food embodies our sacred relationship with the natural world. One manifestation of the re-inhabiting of our land base is by recognizing that sacred relationship and taking steps to undermine the economic and cultural forces that would defile that relationship in the name of financial profit. The process of decolonizing our communities begins with identifying "foodsheds" – taking back our food sovereignty – so we can again embrace all the beauty and health that comes from eating wholesome, sustainably produced food.

Throughout this book, I'd like to maintain a vibe that hopefully inspires or empowers you. I'm not calling for revolution, political upheaval, or militant direct action against against Earth abusers in this book. (Maybe the next one.) But every once in a while, a guy's gotta call it like he sees it. And at this point in the book, I need to stop making insinuations and simply and blatantly identify an enemy. It may not be politically correct or jive with Eastern philosophy to draw a line and declare such an enemy. But in this case, there *is* an enemy that not only needs, but deserves, to be dismantled because the threat it causes to biodiversity and to this planet's inhabitants is of such severe magnitude. It's a big one – the food-industrial complex. The corporate control of our food system is leading us down a very treacherous road.

There are many ways to take down an adversary. But this isn't *The Art of War*. (However, that would be a good idea for a book too.) An enemy can be outright demolished with force, or simply deprived of fuel, rendering it debilitated and ineffective to the point that it becomes irrelevant. I would try not to judge any tactics as they relate to the defense of the lives of all my relations – be they honeybees, black bears, or my children – when those lives are on the line. But whether because of naivety, cowardice, strategy, or some combination thereof, I choose to advocate starving the monster, at least for our purposes here.

In order to do that, the monster first needs to be identified and exposed. But though we need to understand where we came from and how this nightmare came to be, it doesn't do us a lot of practical good now to point our fingers at ancient men who sowed fields of barley in the Middle East 10,000 years ago.

In the interest of fairness, those early agriculturists knew not the consequences of what they were doing. They could have never possibly foreseen the momentous chain of events that would land us *here*. But here we are in the twenty-first century. And the agriculturists today, who sit in air-conditioned meeting rooms, contemplating international market conditions and biosecurity, developing menacing farm bills, they know what's up. They see the continuation of this horror, so much worse than the residents of Jericho could have possibly imagined. These guys know the health crisis we face. They know the environmental tragedies we've inherited. They know about famine, cancer, rampant animal abuse, children dying of mad cow disease and other forms of suffering too long to list here.

These folks know the consequences of their actions and proceed regardless. The pathological managers of meat packing plants and animal factories do not need, nor are they entitled to, our attempts at education. Unlike the ancient farmers of the Fertile Crescent, these people are here, now, committing heinous crimes. I don't know how they can do it, but I know they need to be stopped. There's a lot of talk about so-called sustainable foods, but not enough about food security and what needs to happen to attain it.

By now, I can almost guarantee if you're reading this, you've heard about how your food travels, on average, 1500 miles to reach your mouth. I wouldn't be surprised if you're already well versed on the dangers of genetically modified food. About grain fed to cattle. Pesticides. Herbicides. Abusive working conditions. Global food consuming healthy topsoil, clean water, fossil fuels. In fact, this kind of information is often fed to consumers as a marketing strategy for industrial organic food. The question I have is: can we take this information to the next level? Nearly all of us would starve to death if there were no industrial food system. Not because there isn't food all around, but because we believe we are completely and utterly dependent. And we are, unless we begin to regain skills and a vision that were misplaced generations ago.

How can we possess food security when, in a relatively slow and stealthy way since the industrial revolution, corporations have gained control over our very culture? Not just the food we eat, but our *whole culture.* Not that civilization was ever a worthwhile experiment anyway, but it has gotten a whole lot worse over the last 150 years. In that time, crafty advertisers have figured out how to sell us on corporate agendas that render us all but helpless. Look around. I defy you to deny that our beliefs, behaviors, and possessions are molded by corporations. We are the first people in the *history of the earth* whose culture has been created by corporate entities rather than human beings – for the purpose of driving profits rather than transmitting a rich way of life to our offspring. And the only reason they can get away with such a crime is because of our compliance.

Like I said, I'd really prefer to keep a positive tone here, but it's all rather pathetic, don't you think?

The price we pay as a result of supporting a globalized food system is astounding. Not only is there the environmental cost of mass animal torture, monocropping and chemical agriculture, the health care costs of consuming crappy food, transportation costs, world hunger, military occupation and conquest, but we've very literally lost a fundamental part of who we are as human beings. The expense is nearly impossible to get one's head around. But nonetheless we partake. We concede. We give these bastards the green light. And for what? A bit of convenience? Not only this, but *each and every one of us is capable of learning these skills and building local food systems which are immeasurably more nourishing on every level.*

The fact is that we've lost control of the food supply to entities that are corrupt for *no good reason*. Large-scale, alien operations, subsidized by the government, grow products that resemble and kinda-sorta function like food, and we go ahead and buy it. As a result, we as a society, have become sedentary, apathetic, and frankly incompetent in many ways. We weren't even aware it was happening, but I assure you, we are suffering for it. Come on, don't be offended now. It is vital for our offspring and theirs, to relearn the skills needed to feed themselves. If we do not have food security, then we are already dead. Sure, we can drive to the grocery store *today* for a loaf of bread and jar of peanut butter. We will probably be able to do this tomorrow too. But even *if* we can drive to that store for the rest of our lives whenever we are hungry, there's no saying that we should. Or that there isn't a more fulfilling way to acquire our nutrients.

Moreover, a day will come when our descendants will not be able to have the same conveniences that cheap oil has afforded the past few generations. One day, in the not-so-distant future, grocery stores as we know them and the foreign, processed foods that line their shelves, will cease to exist and humans will live in an uncivilized way again. There are ecological laws that ensure this. (Please, oh please, before that happens, may the gods guide some genius to figure out how to grow coconuts and chocolate in Upstate New York!)

The uncomfortable fact is that we need to concern ourselves with issues of food sovereignty and TEK if we care for our children's future. Decide how you want to be connected to that which sustains you. Is it of more value to be integrated into your community and land base, or have the cheapest food possible? Is it more appropriate to see the land as a resource or as a source of connection to your ancestors? Do you believe that you have a right to self (and community) determination; survival, dignity, and well-being? If so, then as your eyes become unclouded, you may begin to see globalized corporate food for the unstable danger that it is.

You may even begin to see that bioregionalism is the only path to food security.

Once we begin to think bioregionally about food, we begin to apply the concept in ways beyond prediction. We have a new frame of reference, based on proven ancestral ways. At the very least, we transform our relationship with the stuff we put into our bodies and begin to honor the sanctity of food, especially that of animal flesh. This is a logical extension of local, seasonal food. We begin to slow down global institutions that don't serve us. We realize the earth does not *need* our saving, and our civilization does not *deserve* our saving. But, if you want to make a sincere difference in your level of contentment and the lives of countless beings around you, there is no better place to start than with your own body, the land upon which you stand, and the relationship between the two.

***

One of the many reasons I am advocating bioregionalism in this book is because it is a proactive, as opposed to reactive, collection of views. It is an innovative vision in the context of our culture. Bioregionalism aims to create local economies. It connects sustainability with a land base, rather than some abstract global idea. Just as importantly, it honors the native humans that lived in that particular ecosystem. It isn't either antagonistic or defensive in nature because it doesn't rely upon the exploitative strategy of Western civilization for fuel. Not merely as an alternative to a destructive civilization, bioregionalism exists as a healthy system in and of itself.

That being said, something beautiful does happen as a side effect when people choose to embrace and apply bioregionalism. The global capitalist monsters that make us believe we are dependent on them, poisoning the world in the process, begin to weaken as our communities regain vitality. We learn to survive and thrive, while they suffer with failed attempts, trying to desperately usurp and sell what we create. When we relearn ancestral skills and become intimate with local environments, we have no need for global economic agendas. When we attain food sovereignty, they lose leverage and could eventually, just maybe, wither away into irrelevance. Bioregionalism is one thing I fail to see how they can capitalize.

There is overwhelming evidence that suggests I can write this today because of a process our scientists call evolution. Though, by this point in this book, you might *rather* me be an ancient single cell microbe swimming around in a toxic pool. Myself, I'm fond of the process. It's a powerful process. So powerful, so successful in fact, that I suggest we begin cooperating with it like our pre-agricultural species always has. Bioregionalism is in cooperation with evolution. Eating meat is cooperating with evolution. Becoming students of ancestral food knowledge is cooperating with evolution. Thinking we are the pinnacle of creation is *not*. Dismiss my radical ecological viewpoints if you will, but it's harder for most in our scientifically minded society to argue with evolutionary biology.

Most of us modern folk live in a fairy tale that tells us the resources we gobble up to fuel our lifestyle come out of thin air. I do like a good fairy tale, but not the kind that causes us to act pathologically, eviscerating the ground that sustains us. We're spoiled rotten. Johnny Environmentalist drives to his local food coop and "Ban Hydrofracking" meetings in his Prius. But on his way, he filled up his tank from a magic gas pump, the whole while ensuring that dangerous pollution and political upheaval is occurring in less privileged nations *elsewhere*. To be more fair, it's not all Johnny Environmentalist's fault. At least he has good intentions of living less destructively unlike many people out there. After all, there are institutions out there that ensure we *stay* spoiled rotten. So, let's not just pick on Johnny. We could just as easily pick on Brad Bioregionalist who goes to Walmart to get his son snow pants and picks up a couple bunches of bananas before he gets home to write his book about local food. Nah, let's not do that.

The truth is, we don't often have a list of affordable alternative choices. We're born into a messed up world where our options are few. It's designed to be this way by people whose vision is clouded with dreamy images of crisp cash – cash that cannot be eaten when this whole illusion ends. So, it doesn't usually occur to us to think about what our great grandkids will eat and where they'll get food from. For now, we live in a prosperous nation after all.

This is the danger of globalism. Out of sight, out of mind. Not in my backyard. Perhaps if we DID get our energy from our own backyard, we'd be more concerned about how it affects the ecology of *this* place. This is very much analogous to how we acquire our food. If the countryside where I live was saturated for miles upon miles with monocrop banana plantations and my groundwater was saturated with toxic chemicals from pesticide runoff as a result, I probably wouldn't buy those bananas. And if we got our meat from our backyard, we'd be much more concerned with how that animal was treated and if it was clean and healthy. Globalism is an environmental threat. Likewise, global food and global environmentalism are environmental threats regardless of intentions to the contrary. Local economies, complete with neighbors producing and feeding themselves and each other, are the affordable alternatives.

Perhaps we need not "begin" anything new at all. We don't need to reinvent the wheel. There are no fancy technological or political solutions that await us. We just need to simply return to a path that we've always had access to, if we could just shift our perspective of the world and our role within it.

Based on historical fact (or prehistorical fact if you choose to differentiate), I could make a strong case for animism, or for tribalism, or for breastfeeding for that matter – all of which would be a boon to our collective well-being. What is relevant is when something is out of sorts, the evidence is incredibly substantial to support the notion that it's a good idea to pay attention to the workings of your bioregion and act accordingly. Call it TEK, deep ecology, primitivism, or the delusions of a hunter-gatherer wannabe trying to write a book when he should be sleeping. It doesn't matter.

Modern meat production is still disgustingly cruel and the cause for gross pollution. The animal flesh most people consume is tainted and unhealthy. Nonetheless, humans are a species that evolved eating meat, and we wouldn't have made it this damn far if the preceding facts had always been true.

Which means, there *is* a better way.

And I've made it a personal mission to try to find it.

5. BIRTHRIGHT

"You have to listen and observe … that is the most important thing."

Sepp Holzer

I am the proud father of two amazing young boys, amazingly obsessed with lethal weaponry in all its forms. At the time of writing this, these kids have a veritable arsenal of weapons from knives to machetes, throwing stars to bows and BB guns. They even asked for a sword for Christmas and I happily obliged. (They didn't ask for *The Moosewood Cookbook*.) Since what would commonly be considered preschool age, both of these boys have often spent significant portions of their days carving sticks into spears.

At our old place of residence, we had a sizable vegetable garden, which is the equivalent of saying that we had a sizable mammalian pest problem. One of these creatures – a fat kale and broccoli filled woodchuck – took up residence under a woodpile in the corner of our yard where he could be close to the action. One day our oldest son, who was six at the time, decided he wanted to be a little helper like many children his age. His contribution was an offer to kill the woodchuck. I can still see the excitement in his wide, bloodthirsty eyes – the pride in himself that he had come up with such a brilliant plan. That morning, he took some time to carve the perfect spear. Somehow, the thirty others strewn across the porch and the yard would not suffice for the all-important job at hand.

He spent the better part of an afternoon crouched, belly down, upon the top of that woodpile. Spear in hand. Cocked and ready for that woodchuck to come out from underneath. His eyes fixated. His body still. I can tell you from personal experience, and if you have children you might agree, there are not many activities that would captivate a six-year-old boy enough to sit that still and silent for that amount of time. In his six-year-old mind, he wanted that kill. And he wanted it badly. This is the same boy I've seen driven to teary eyes at the sight of one of his peers needlessly squashing spiders. I'm the type that looks at that sort of behavior as somewhat peculiar, and must ask myself, "why?"

The answer, of course, is because of instinct.

***

Others would surely disagree. Back in my vegan days, I knew a couple of women that were proponents of an ecofeminist philosophy. If you've never heard of such a thing, ecofeminism is a movement that suggests that the subordination of women and nature are one in the same. For the record, I believe they are on to something. Something important. Unfortunately, then they trip over their own sense of self-admiration and thus miss a big chunk of historical and anthropological evidence that they otherwise might have come to.

Among other faulty conclusions, more often than not, veganism is espoused as an inseparable component of ecofeminist ethics. Having been a vegan for so long, with a predominantly herbivorous friend base, this is how I became introduced to the idea that the oppression of women and the oppression of the natural world are connected. But according to ecofeminism, hunting is simply another form of domination, an equivalent to rape. Men are insecure and callous, so they kill animals and rape women for the same gratification.

According to an ecofeminist perspective, my children's fascination with spears and arrows and playing predator are not normal; they are perverse and will inevitably lead to a detestation of females. Forget that these two little boys love and are fascinated with all that is the outdoors. Forget that most all their friends are little girls whom they worship along with the ground they walk on. What is apparently an intrinsic certainty, by virtue of the fact that they are males, because they lack the ability to bear children, they will jealously act out in destructive ways towards both animals and women. Okay.

Jim Mason, in his book, *An Unnatural Order*, echoes the ecofeminist perspective by claiming "primal men had feelings of gender insecurity and lack of status in the group," and asserts that the development of hunting was a means of "compensating" born from jealousy. This, of course, is reactionary absurdity. He claims that the role of hunting has been exaggerated by male writers, male scientists, male anthropologists, male hunters, and male men of all sorts. Through the eyes of someone with this perspective, every bit of important anthropological evidence that has been uncovered by males is tainted with chauvinism and thus apparently not valid. Despite any lack of meaningful evidence, throughout the book, Mason asserts over and over that hunting is a mere 20,000 years old, which is simply a fabrication. Despite the fact that he's completely wrong, I'm not trying to pick on Jim here; the guy has contributed positively to the debate about food choices. But to me, it is scary that this type of information is taken as gospel by impressionable people who don't know better.

Sorry ladies (and Jim Mason), but hunting in and of itself, *in no way, shape, or form* necessarily leads to the domination of women. Contrarily, the evidence says the exact opposite. Far from teaching callousness and cruelty, hunting teaches sensitivity, compassion and patience. Killing is not perverse, it is essential to life. When we gave up hunting as a subsistence strategy, and replaced it with agriculture, it is then that men began subjugating women on a wholesale basis. Agriculture and settlement are the necessary roots of domination and patriarchy.

As stated previously, hunter-gatherer cultures – while certainly having some variability in social organization – tend to have a few things in common, such as an animist cosmology, TEK, and a largely egalitarian relationship with each other. Because men often hunted and women gathered, work was shared amongst the entire community. Division of labor between the sexes simply did not equate with stratification in status in these societies.

Women were revered as the givers of life and often played a central role in creation legends. Females occupied a central position within tribes and matrilineal systems among indigenous people were not uncommon. There would have been *no benefit* for males to attempt to dominate its very life support system and vice versa, so male and female energy generally remained balanced. Our success through hundreds of thousands of years of evolution affirms that hunting is not correlated with sexism. It couldn't have been.

While the work of both men and women was equally important in hunter-gatherer societies, leading to cooperation and mutual respect, agricultural settlements demolished such arrangements. Agriculture led to the creation of the concepts of property, possession, and class. Now, the work of a few could provide food for all and the division of labor was altered in a way that twisted male-female relations. The value of women and the feminine were necessarily reduced. A new focus on the possession of wealth and the defense of that wealth turned women into second-class citizens.

In other words, women enjoyed dignity when their men were hunters. And both genders worked and played equally to feed the community. When their men became farmers, there was a rise in gender stratification and females were reduced to a position of inferiority. Contrary to the baseless assertions of ecofeminists and the like who wish to bash hunting, the *decline* in hunting due to agriculture is the root of the domination of females. Either way, there is no doubt that now we live in society where gender stratification is significant and it is usually women who are the disadvantaged. And there is also no doubt of the severity of our environmental predicament. In order to re-establish an egalitarian relationship with each other and the land, both genders need to look to their ancestral roots for wisdom.

***

Richard Manning writes in *Against the Grain* "When a woman ambles through the Union Square market and the deep purple glint of a plum catches her eye, she is replicating a primal process, awakening pathways of primal signals. The process itself is satisfying, human."

I don't know that I could have articulated this better. Manning is not the only one to observe this phenomenon as it applies to women. I have read more than one interpretation explaining the stereotypical desire to shop that many modern women experience as a warped manifestation of deep, ancient urges relating to foraging.

Chellis Glendinning, one of the pioneer writers in the growing field of ecopsychology, explains in her book *My Name is Chellis and I'm in Recovery from Western Civilization* of her own healing after a lifetime of abuse and detachment, ultimately prompted by an acceptance of herself as a "gatherer." She finds what she calls enlightenment in foraging wild mushrooms in the mountains. Suggestion after suggestion from books and magazines that discuss solutions to our disconnection from the natural world commonly note that harvesting and preparation of wild edibles is one remedy to our predicament.

I myself can testify to the powerful experience of foraging. It is deeply satisfying to be able to identify plants, become familiar with them and harvest from them. To make wild leek and garlic mustard pesto, sassafras root beer, stinging nettle frittata, steamed Japanese knotweed … as Chellis says, it *is* enlightening in a way. My kids forage on wild grapes, wood sorrel, cattail pollen, and hawthorn berries without a second thought, and I believe they are better off for it. But the fact remains that this scene is largely promoted by women. This makes perfect sense of course, as more and more female naturalists are accepting the notion that gathering is a legacy of our ancestral mothers and sisters, thus learning and passing down these skills. Certainly any of us, including myself, can benefit from the practice of gathering plants. In the same way there are some awesome female hunters out there. But in my experience, women are usually first to realize that they have much to gain from dabbling in foraging and studying herbalism.

I know of several wilderness skills organizations that offer classes with clever names such as "Sisters of the Forest," "Plant Medicine Retreat," "Women of the Forest" or "Autumn Woods Knitting Retreat." These various nature retreats are designed specifically for women and usually involve ceremony, circles, foraging, nature crafts, and various other activities to nurture the power and beauty within. Their purpose is to honor and support femininity through connection with the land and each other. These types of programs are nothing less than admirable, if not essential, tools towards the long deserved re-empowerment of women in our culture. They help introduce women to their heritage as healers, nurturers, and cherished pillars of the community. It is essential for any prescription for a sustainable future that we re-establish the honorable role of of all that is feminine in a thriving society.

That being recognized, it then can be said that there is to Yin without Yang. There is no light without darkness. No Lita Ford without Ozzy Osbourne. The masculine and feminine are beautifully intertwined. They are equal and complimentary forces that together, and only together, make up a whole, balanced, dynamic system. They are both essential. In fact, they are completely interdependent. Thus it follows that efforts to connect modern women with their primal alter egos, without our culture simultaneously exploring what that means for men as well, is an exercise in futility.

While femininity has been grossly defiled and women have been systematically dis-empowered by our patriarchal society, the domestication process has taken a toll on men as well. We have been born into a culture where healthy and sustainable models of manhood are all but nonexistent. As men, we are compelled to embrace the conventional interpretation of masculinity that is unjust and oppressive in too many ways to list here. Or, it sometimes seems the only other option is to surrender to misandry, or at least an overly soft and disparaging view of our own very nature. The so-called privileges we supposedly inherited as men have made us more confused and as lost as ever. Yet, the forest and savanna and their inhabitants belong to no man or women and in fact, their wisdom has been shared with *both* genders for millions of years if we would only attempt to listen.

I am not unaware that issues such as gender roles, genetic predispositions and whether a hunting-gathering dichotomy even exists are sensitive and complicated issues. But I still contend that there needs to be an accurate (rather than politically correct) assessment of our historical and anthropological life as non-civilized males and females in order to begin to heal our fractured relationship to the natural world. As a male trying to healthily make my way within a very confused and convoluted excuse for a culture, I am left asking – what examples do *we* have? Which avenues do *we* as males walk to mend our disintegrated sense of place in the world? Don't we *all* deserve better than these cards we've been dealt?

Those kinds of questions and honest assessments of our evolutionary history unquestionably point to men as remarkably non-aggressive and reverent hunters. What kind of profound impact could this realization have if combined with the empowerment of women, as both genders try to emulate the relationship our tribal ancestors had with each other and the land? While we need not necessarily divide labor or organize our society after any particular land-based culture, the guidance offered to us by our egalitarian ancestors is essential as we carve a new path.

Let us hop in the old DeLorean again, and this time, let us travel a hell of lot longer back than a mere 10,000 years ago to the dawn of totalitarian agriculture.

If the history of the universe was laid out into a calendar year and we were at the very end, the first hominids did not appear until the last few hours, modern humans not until the last few minutes, and agriculturists only a couple seconds ago. Evolution of life on Earth began some four billion years ago. The first apes appeared 23 million years ago. It is difficult to conceptualize this quantity of time in which we have evolved. But what is clear is that in relation to the evolution of life on Earth, we civilized folk are a mere speck in the process.

So fire up the flux capacitor and let's take a glimpse of what our ancient ancestors were up to all those years before they began toiling all day in fields of domesticated grasses. Before kingdoms, war, Viagra, and American Idol. I understand it may seem to the untrained eye that I'm just rambling haphazardly back and forth between time periods. But, in the movies, they call this style of storytelling *nonlinear narrative*. Yeah, that's it.

***

Did you know at one time, hundreds of thousands of years ago, there were multiple species of hominids in the genus "Homo," some living simultaneously? That's right, some anthropologists estimate anywhere from six to as many as 14 species of humans have walked the earth at various times. It's kind of like today we have multiple species of rabbits hopping around the world. And actually *Homo sapiens* and Neanderthals are more closely related than the cottontail rabbits and snowshoe hares found in my home state today.

Well, even Bugs Bunny and his cousins have to make a living somehow, and being so closely related, all having come from a similar lineage, they all happen to be herbivores. Out of the many species of rabbits across the world, they all nonetheless have virtually the same eating habits. Rabbits graze on the herbaceous plants and grasses found in the different bioregions in which they inhabit. There's that word again.

Likewise, all of these species of hominids made their living in very similar ways – by foraging and yes, hunting. For more than 99 percent of our hominid history, our ancestors survived by eating wild game to one degree or another. It may have been horses in what is now known as Spain, or baboons in what is now known as Kenya. Either way, animals have been an important food source in our development as a species and there were no factory farms during the Pleistocene. I think Elmer Fudd would be proud.

How far back do I need to go to make a convincing argument? Certainly farther than the 20,000 years Jim Mason likes to go. How about around *four million years ago!* Our first and most distinguishing attribute that separates us from our primate cousins is the fact that we walk on two legs. This is an adaptation called bipedalism, and before this, we hung in the trees with the other apes doing the arboreal thing. Though not of the *Homo* genus, these bipedal apes are our ancestors, a point in our family tree. There were several species of these walking ape-like hominids, the details aren't important here. What is important to my point is what they ate. And even more importantly, why did they come out of the trees? Our ancestors this far back were quite effectively adapted for a life in the trees. Not to mention all the big predator cats and other dangers out on the savannah who would gobble up a defenseless little ape without second thought. There must have been a good motivator to come down on the ground and walk around.

There are several overlapping models to account for the evolution of primate bipedalism, and acting together probably contributed to the emergence of the hominid lineage. But one that would be hard to deny is that while they were beginning to walk upright habitually across the plains of Africa, they were scavenging on carrion. I know I feel better in the morning after feasting on some remnants of partially decomposed antelope. Lion leftovers are delectable, and maybe an *Australopithecus* ape-man wanted to service his lady interest by bringing her some meat, being that she was so busy with the new baby and all. Being upright allowed him to scout farther, keep an eye out for danger, and carry food with greater efficiency. Anthropologists have debated for nearly a century as to whether these particular primates hunted, and I won't necessarily make that claim (though logic dictates it's likely). There is strong evidence that our earliest bipedal ancestors ate predominately plant material. After all, humans still do. Plants have nutrients. Plants are good. I like salads too. But, it is perfectly reasonable to assume that nutritionally dense and easily digestible meat nonetheless played an important role in the development of bipedalism and thus our very evolution as a species.

While I won't make the claim that Lucy and her friends were chasing down zebras across the savannah with antelope horns as daggers three million years ago, I will make a very definite claim, that easily by a million years ago, our ancestors were bona fide hunters. *Homo erectus* was the species that colonized new continents, learned to control fire, and partook in coordinated, premeditated, cooperative hunts for big game. Cattle, horses, rhinoceroses, elephants, antelopes, boars, elephants. Elephants? If humans were hunting *elephants* a million years ago, then it is safe to assume they were hunting smaller, more readily kill-able animals long before that. In fact, earlier *Homo* species had learned to use stone tools to carve meat and bones off of carcasses by two million years ago and were also likely hunting, at least for a small proportion of their diet. Brains were getting bigger. Our ancestors, thanks to a healthy diet of meat and plants now, were becoming more intelligent. More creative. Tracking animals. Reading the landscape. Remembering the routes and timing of migrations. I find it utterly fascinating, don't you?

Homo erectus dominated the human family tree for nearly a million and a half years before they went extinct only about 200,000 years ago. Due to their increased brain size, they developed hundreds of cultures, tools, and traditions dependent upon various environments. They foraged and hunted lands in Africa, Europe, and Asia. Human species that evolved simultaneously and after them, like all those rabbits mentioned above, shared similar subsistence strategies. *Homo antecessor* hunted. *Homo heidelbergensis* hunted. *Homo neanderthalensis* hunted.

And if this wasn't convincing enough, despite not being *nearly* as closely related to us as the aforementioned hominid species, chimpanzees and bonobos are nearly 99 percent like us modern humans in genetic makeup – and they aren't extinct. Our lineages may have separated millions of years ago, but they're the closest animals to us alive today – physically, genetically, and behaviorally. Damn close as a matter of fact. Close enough to observe, in order to gather a bit more evidence into our own heritage.

Chimpanzees get a bad rap. Observed chimp tendencies towards violence and aggression are often used as models to explain depraved human behavior and to justify cruelty or warfare as a normal part of human nature. It's not hard to find information that claims aggressive or even vicious behavior is typical of most primates, and it's usually the chimps that are used as examples. Recent evidence suggests however that it is population pressure due to loss of habitat that influences these types of behaviors. It's a bit more understandable to put chimp aggression in its proper context – as a pathological response to unnatural conditions, loss of resources and habitat. Either way, chimpanzees can be intelligent, cooperative, and personable. They also regularly hunt pigs, antelopes, baboons and other monkeys. Hunts that involve teamwork and patience.

And who can find fault with the bonobo, the hippie of the primate world? Arguably, more closely related to us than any other animal on the face of the planet. Everyone loves the peaceful, tolerant, free-loving bonobos. Unlike their chimpanzee cousins, bonobos are known for being gentle and sociable, not to mention sexy. They have sex of all kinds for any excuse they can come up with. They're nurturing and kind to one another. So, with all these admirable characteristics, let's not forget to mention that they also *hunt*. The peaceful ape – the flower child of the jungle – hunts squirrels, rodents, forest antelopes and even monkeys and, not only that, has been known to rip them apart and eat them alive.

Perhaps multiple human species over hundreds upon hundreds of thousands of years feeding themselves by hunting and gathering isn't enough to convince you of the substantial role hunting has had on the development of our bodies and minds. Perhaps studies of our closest living relatives aren't compelling enough. Well, let's just take a look at the only hominid left standing.

***

Homo sapiens. Anatomically modern humans. Us.

I have held an actual cast of a *Homo erectus* skull in my hands, and I'm betting most people reading this would be hard pressed to notice much of a difference between it and a modern human skull. And for 98 percent of people, over 98 percent shared DNA with a bonobo just isn't high enough for them to take interest. These facts boggle my mind. But then again, we've already established that I'm not normal. Either way, if you're not interested in looking at early hominids or other apes, fine. But you just can't deny what our own kind has been doing for a few hundred thousand years.

Modern humans arose in Africa and have been walking and hunting the planet for some 300,000 years. Significant progress in the realm of technological sophistication becomes more evident in the fossil record of this period – fueled, once again, by hunting. From this time up until the Neolithic Revolution, there was a consistent increase in the refinement of tools as well as in the number of prey species exploited by humans, not to mention the specifics of the evolution of more efficient hunting strategies. By this time, we see undeniable evidence of communal hunts and the remains of countless big game prey species. These include woolly mammoths, woolly rhinos, and all sorts of other good tasting woolly animals. Our *Homo sapiens* ancestors, using the most workable way of feeding themselves that humankind has ever known, spread to every continent on the planet and did so sustainably. If there are answers to our current predicament, who has them? Not PETA. Not the ecofeminists. I'd ask the people who, by far, have the most successful track record.

While modern hunter-gatherers cannot be seen as carbon copies of our ancient relatives due to a variety of factors, not the least of which is often some contact with the industrial world, they do share a common livelihood. One that cannot be ignored when discussing what a sustainable food system might look like. All across the world, where they still exist, exiled by Western civilization to marginal lands, indigenous people *still* hunt a proportion of their food. Whether it be the San of southern Africa, the Inuit of the Arctic regions, the Yanomami and other tribes of the Amazon, the many tribes of Papua New Guinea, the secluded Indians of Peru … they are hunters and gatherers and gardeners. We need to ask ourselves, what characteristics are shared by all human life, as opposed to those that are a result of social conditioning?

The truth is, we don't know a heck of a lot about the complex day to day lives of Paleolithic humans. There were fluctuations in climate and a variety of habitats that our ancestors had to adapt to, as wide as the earth itself. Logic dictates there must have been profound cultural differences from tribe to tribe and region to region. But there are a few things we do know. One of those, like it or not, is that natural selection, a process nearly all sane people can agree upon, has favored human adaptations for hunting. Whether we physically need to hunt for survival is not the relevant question. In light of the predicaments we face, the question is: what is the context in which we humans are at our optimal level of physical and mental health?

What the evidence indicates is that hunting, and in turn the consumption and digesting of animal flesh, is a defining human trait honed by millions of years of evolution.

***

So far, in this chapter, I have made the case that hunting has historically been an integral part of the human experience for well over a million (if not *millions* of) years. This fact can be, and has been, deduced by examining piles upon piles of biological and anthropological evidence. But, even I will be the first to say that this evidence is insufficient in ways. I *know* that humanity has been sculpted for tens of thousands of generations by interdependence and interaction with the natural environment. I *know*, without a shadow of a doubt, that we have always lived within an environmental context and this context has shaped our bodies, our behaviors, our thoughts, and our cultures. I *know*, not only because I read it in a science textbook, but because, as a person who reveres the value of habitat, I find it intuitive.

Such experience brings us to an aspect of our existence that goes deeper than what can be tested in a laboratory. I feel another slippery slope coming, but I nonetheless have to ask the question. Why is it not foolish to believe that scientifically-defined human senses constitute the limit of our abilities of perception? In other words, what makes us think that we have the authority to maintain only that which can be measured is the be-all, end-all of what exists within our natural environment? Even ecology is now an accepted scientific study of the connections between living organisms and the environment. But as with all things that are connected, there must be a force or forces that connect.

Now I'm not a religious person. Most of this modern world's hierarchical, salvationist religions thrive on the exploitation of nearly an entire world of spiritually lost and broken individuals. I figure if grasshoppers, wildebeests, and blue jays don't need church, I sure as hell don't. But there is something to be said that it is almost universal that aboriginal cultures, for all their countless differences, have a shared diametrically opposing cosmology to that of our own. Why do land-based cultures everywhere, almost without exception, believe that the universe is alive with potent non-human spiritual forces than cannot be separated from the physical world?

There are a lot of negative stereotypes about hunters in this country. There are a lot of accusations of violations of various kinds. And it may be true that there is a small proportion of irresponsible and even callous animal murderers out there, cloaked in beer-soaked camo and calling themselves "hunters." But the fact is that there are millions of hunters in this country alone. And perhaps surprisingly, even in this spiritually bankrupt culture, a survey examining the role of hunting in human development found that the majority of them still thank the animal, and/or some higher power, after making a kill. Hunting leads to inner peace, patience, and self-esteem. And in my experience, the reverence for nature that hunters hold within absolutely defies many of the stereotypes.

After hundreds of thousands of years, hunting *still* taps into something sacred in the majority of cases. I feel safe making the generalization that the emotional and spiritual experience of hunting remains the same whether it is done with a modern compound bow engineered to precision or a Stone Age spear. It is an occasion of knowing *something* wise and wild. It is primal. This is only something that can be understood on a deeper level. There are not many activities that make one wake up out of a warm, cozy bed at some ungodly hour in order to go shiver and freeze in the woods. I am certainly not a morning person, but for some mysterious reason, there is one time a year I actually look forward to this. Like sexual drives that move otherwise sane people to partake in so-called deranged, uncivilized behavior, hunting is clearly instinct. Perhaps even untamable. I have felt it, along with millions of my ancestors and probably millions of others even in the twenty-first century. Therefore, I know it is woven into our fabric as humans.

And so I make the case that hunting is divine. Like cougars or coyotes or chimpanzees, it is our gift. It is honest in an otherwise dishonest world. Yes, we have hunted first and foremost to feed our families and communities. But in the process, our senses evolved in relation to the hunt. Our psyches evolved in relation to the hunt. This is the biology our scientists speak of. But let's not dismiss that, just just as certainly, our very soul evolved in relation to the hunt as well as our relation to other unidentifiable entities.

This is why hunting stories have been an important element of entertaining ourselves throughout the history of human culture, and is still so today when people get together in modern times. This is why cave art of the European Upper Paleolithic revolved around majestic animals and their pursuit. It has been suggested that these so-called primitive paintings were done by artists performing *magic*. Perhaps this is why the style and beauty that characterizes these paintings has baffled many modern artists and captivated onlookers since they were discovered. Likewise, throughout the ages, humans have adorned themselves with necklaces and other jewelry made from teeth and other bones of felled prey. It seems it is human nature, if such a thing exists, to express gratitude and piety towards hunted animals in the form of art and ceremony.

Hunting is a sacred act at its core. In its uncorrupted form, it is honorable. Because we are human, we hunt. Because we hunt, we are human. And this is an evolutionary reality that modern men would do well to embrace within its proper context. This is not to say that men are responsible for the success of our species at the exclusion of females. In fact, in certain places, evidence suggests that women did partake in the hunt. On top of that, what anthropologists often label "gathering" by females in other cultures actually includes the "hunting" of insects, shellfish, grubs, and even small mammals. And even where they didn't hunt, they gathered necessary vegetables *and* likely partook in the skinning, processing, butchering, cooking of the meat, making of clothes from the hide, etc. It is the exuberant, wild man and woman that still resides within each of our psyches that has the best chance of edifying us.

But modern men, in particular, have been dispossessed of our inheritance. And because of this, our society, and the planet itself suffer. *This* is why my boys are fascinated with hunting and weapons, because since the dawn of humanity, in earth-based cultures, hunting has served as a rite of passage from childhood to manhood. It is in their genes. *It is in all of our genes.* Natural selection has favored the egalitarian human hunter/forager. I uphold that sustenance hunting has a very important role to play in moving away from an unsustainable and unhealthy industrialized food system towards a bioregional vision. I know it has for my own path.

***

This chapter could have just as easily been called "A 33-Year-Old Suburban Kid Gets a Gun." At this point in our story, we've not only seen how agriculture betrayed the world, but how this ex-herbivore betrayed the movement he grew up in, alienating himself from people he would otherwise consider allies in the good fight against factory farming. (What a jerk.) But hopefully I can make up for it, by telling a different kind of story. A story of personal growth. A story of betraying the domesticated part of myself that says how much easier it would be to just purchase cheap meat wrapped in cellophane at the grocery store like everyone else. A story that I can only hope gives a little nudge to the non-hunters who can sympathize with this message, but don't think they know how to get off the fence.

I've already mentioned my adolescence and young adult years and the diet I embraced for most of it. What this means is that although I learned how to cook tofu and rice quite proficiently, up until recent years, I didn't know a damn thing about meat. Eventually, my dietary inclinations did evolve past simply abstaining from animal products. I did eventually begin flirting with foraging and dabbling in dumpster diving. So, I wasn't totally uncomfortable eating on the fringes of the food economy. But meat? The flesh of the innocent?

Whether we like it or not, hunting is a logical extension of many of these types of alternative food philosophies, whether they be based on localism, frugality, health, or being more in tune with the cycles of the natural world.

What I haven't mentioned is that growing up, I never went camping, joined the boy scouts, fished or enjoyed much of any outdoor activity at all for that matter. Perhaps like some of you, I certainly didn't grow up with the luxury of being raised in a hunting family. My mother didn't allow candles in the house, let alone a gun. What this all means is that for most of my life, I didn't even know what a deer track looked like, let alone how to successfully find and turn a wild animal into dinner. I knew how to make a mean split pea soup. I knew how to steal food from Whole Foods. I even knew how to make stinging nettle juice. But with hunting, I was on my own. I knew the "why." But I had to figure out the "how," "when," and "where" all by my lonesome.

Hunting as a sacred rite of passage as I have described it above is not simply some romantic concept, it is nearly universal in non-civilized cultures. (In fact, forget romance, I want grilled venison loin steaks. Hell yeah.) But nonetheless, we just can't ignore the reality that most men in our culture are deprived of any semblance of such a ritual, and so we grow up lost and confused and unclear on what it means to be a man. We grow up either vegetarian like myself, or worse – eating fatty, corn-fed beef burgers and nasty hot dogs bought at some warehouse retail club by our wives. Though it came twenty years too late, in 2009, I was able to experience this transformation and there are no words in the English language to relay my gratitude for it.

But like I said, I had no uncle that took me into the woods with a .22. I had no friends that hunted. No mentor. I didn't know about guns, about regulations and what licenses were required. I knew I would stick out like a sore thumb at a shooting range. So how does it happen that a guy who has been arrested several times in the name of animal defense finds himself sitting silently in the woods, doing some pre-season scouting before his first hunting season, visualizing taking the life of one of these beautiful creatures walking past fifteen yards away?

I simply made a choice to embrace my birthright, did some research, and at the risk of sounding hokey, put my intentions out into the universe. And the gods, knowing I had not yet experienced the savory pleasure that is deer liver for breakfast, and who I assume prefer things a certain way, answered accordingly.

Actually, Fred answered accordingly. A man who was famous among local foodies for raising the best organic chickens in the area and being a little eccentric, two facts that I would later be able to attest to. However, this is not about Fred's chickens, it is about his enthusiasm in playing a role in converting an ex-vegan into a sharpshooter. See, at one point, I had asked Fred for some input or advice on purchasing a firearm. And any excuse to take a break from the all day laborious job of farming, especially if it involved *guns*, got the man excited. A man like this considers it his duty as a sportsman to pass on the tradition. Its not like I was going to take advantage of this fact. But I wasn't going to refuse the aid of someone so excited to help me either. A vegan for 12 years? I needed all the help I could get.

I visited Fred's farm on a several occasions. He'd rant about politics, I'd listen while I helped him move some wood or rotate the cattle. Eventually, we'd fire guns. And he had a lot. A lot of guns. A lot of stories. A lot of opinions. I was appreciative to have his time and use of his land to practice. This was the summer before I shot my first deer.

It was on the last day of hunting season. I wasn't even going to go out that day, as I had spent so much time in the woods that autumn. I had seen deer, but it was more about practice, about being comfortable in this new role. It was my first year attempting to hunt, and I really felt (as I still do), that simply being out in the woods with a weapon did not entitle me to succeed.

I had no expectations – in fact I had all but given up by that point in the fall – but not ten minutes after I got out of the car on the last morning of the season, I had placed a perfect shot to her vitals. She fell and died near instantaneously. I took a short walk, trembling through the snowy woods and came back. I'm not typically sensitive to these sorts of things, but as I knelt over her, I thanked her while touching her still warm body, and I could almost feel that animal's energy redirect into my own.

Hunting necessarily puts a limitation on one's ability to feel superior over other life forms. It is very difficult not to appreciate a creature that has such a superior sense of smell, grace, and speed. Hunting invokes a sense of respect and peace. For many years, I had attempted to cleanse myself of any notion of human superiority over other animals. It wasn't until that moment that any remnants of that ugly myth were fully exposed.

I had become a hunter.

After gutting it with my dull Mora survival knife, I dragged that deer to my car, put it in my trunk and began driving home. I still remember exactly where I was on that drive when I started getting tears in my eyes. Not sadness. Not happiness. I was just flooded with an unidentifiable emotion. I got home. I skinned it with the same dull survival knife, and my wife and I butchered it up into various cuts, saving the heart for our first meal. I subsequently attempted to brain tan the hide, and my wife made soap for the next year out of its fat. That deer gave me so much more than food for the winter. It was a teacher. And because of this, I could never again view that animal or another as simply a "resource."

This is the sort of reciprocity that has been playing out between hunter and prey for too many ages to count.

I'm not setting out to be overly sentimental here. I don't want to over-dramatize anything. Yet, the truth of the matter is that hunting is a powerful process. It's honest in a way that no conventional meat could ever be. I am trying to get across that a bioregional perspective has such more meaningful effects than just buying locally or eating free-range meat. It is about self discovery. It is about viewing all of us in the community of life as manifestations of the same land base, not as inanimate objects to be exploited.

It is certainly not the only way, but sustenance hunting is one of the most *efficient* means of actualizing this fact.

***

Perhaps I need to offer some clarification to avoid misconception. For my purposes, I choose to describe the process that I am advocating for as *sustenance* hunting. I would personally differentiate between this and what is more commonly referred to as "subsistence hunting." After all, there are many reasons why people, and in particular, men, hunt. As with anything, these motivations range from the unhealthy (competition, machismo, commercial gain, domination) to the healthy (meat, recreation, freedom, insight). Many of these goals can and do overlap; they are not mutually exclusive. I'm not sure of official hunting terminology, and it's really all just a matter of semantics anyway, but when I think of subsistence hunting, I think of survival. There are cultures and families that need to hunt, literally, to survive. Subsistence hunting is what you need to do when your plane crashes into the remote subarctic forests of Alaska. For me, subsistence hunting conjures images of backwoods hermits, or a small family living of the grid someplace in the middle the Canadian Boreal Wilderness. It is too narrow a concept in the context of modernity. It's not what I'm aiming for.

Contrarily, the word "sustenance" invokes a sense of nourishment, a long-term maintaining of a way of life. It implies sustainability. It means living with the land. It suggests to thrive rather than merely survive. In the twenty-first century, most of us do not need to hunt to live. But we do very much need nourishment. And one look around at the general populace will tell anyone with at least one functioning eye that most modern folks aren't getting that.

I may not have years of knowledge to share on the physical art of hunting, but I know enough that I have been forever altered in a positive way by embracing this part of me. Despite the potential for exploitation and ill-intention, and despite the negative popular opinion of hunting, it is nonetheless undeniably our inheritance. It is intensely meaning-ful. For this reason alone, it is worth contemplating.

To take a life in order to give life, from a place of gratitude and respect, has been transformative. And it is this transformation, experienced one way or the other, that is key to the empowerment that will in turn lead to the restoration of healthy community-based food economies. Bioregional economies. And when we cannot or should not hunt, we need not starve. Because luckily, land-based cultures acquired food in other sustainable ways as well.

6. OPPORTUNITY

"If 'wild husbandry' strikes us as a contradiction in terms, then the fault is with us, not the phrase."

Robert Kimber, *Living Wild and Domestic*

Heather Sanford spent much of her young adult life within the same scene of rebellious punk rock kids as I did. She even played bass guitar for a local all-female death metal band. I didn't know her then, as she lived in a different town in Upstate New York. But now, after talking to her and reminiscing about the good old days, I'm sure we probably crossed paths in a mosh pit or two. Maybe I stage dove on her head. It doesn't matter so much anymore what shows we both attended or what bands we liked. What definitely matters now is The Piggery – a "Farm to Table Butcher and Deli" in Ithaca, New York. Heather co-owns the Piggery with her husband Brad and – pardon my French – my whole family is sure as pig shit glad they do.

Here's the embarrassing truth. When I moved to Ithaca, I didn't know about The Piggery. But, I'm confident that if I had found out about it sooner, I would have made the move to this town sooner. Ironically, the most world-famous vegetarian restaurant is also in this city, and it can't hold a match to the greatness of the little, relatively undiscovered deli that Heather and Brad own. As a matter of fact, I can't fathom how such a sizable vegetarian population can even coexist in a town that is home to The Piggery.

So what is The Piggery, other than the most top-notch culinary joint I know? And why does it have any relevance to this book, other than the fact that they sell meat? Well, simply because The Piggery exemplifies many of the points I'm trying to get across in this book. They don't just sell meat as a consumer product in order to make a profit. They raise those pigs themselves with the utmost care, and I would go as far as to say, love. There is no doubt a fondness for their animals and a disgust that anyone could conceive of raising a pig in a crate unable to move. At their deli, they not only sell their own pastured pig products (I'm very close to drooling on the keyboard here thinking of pulled pork burritos), they also have a butcher counter filled with exclusively local, humanely raised chicken, beef, rabbit, etc. The vegetables they use are local and seasonally grown according to environmentally sound principles, as are the pastured eggs and baked goods and dairy products. Not only this, but everything in the deli down to the utensils is either compostable or recyclable.

The farm, the deli, the scrumptious charcuterie – this is just one aspect of what Heather and Brad are doing. They also sometimes travel to teach communities about sustainable agricultural methods and give in-depth demonstrations on how to butcher a pig to homesteaders, urbanites in Brooklyn, and such. Plus, they operate a meat CSA on top of it all!

They're not in it for the money, and in fact don't have much. Partly this is due to the fact that The Piggery is a living-wage employer, offering a living wage to all of their employees from the cooks to the drive-thru attendants to the dishwashers. Mostly, however, they just genuinely love all things pig.

But what is most interesting to me about this story of pure meaty goodness is that for several years, Heather was a vegetarian. Like me, she sang along to all those militant animal rights lyrics and believed in them from the bottom of her heart. But she began to suffer a series of tangible health problems due to an overconsumption of soy. She began to feel better once she incorporated animal products back into her diet, but remained committed to not supporting a factory model of meat production. And then one day, she and Brad bought a pig. She was a punk rocker turned homesteader turned pig farmer. In other words, she didn't stop progressing. She's proud of her journey and what they do for the animals, the land, and the community. And I find that inspiring.

Heather and Brad may not have done so intentionally, but the way in which they are providing meat to this community is compatible with human nature. Their business model, from a certain perspective, is in line with land-based cultures around the world, at least in the sense that it mimics and supports local ecosystems and economies while nourishing the community and the land. While animal husbandry is certainly not as ancient as hunting and gathering, there is certainly something to be said about its place in the solution to our modern predicament – perhaps even more so than hunting itself. What entities such as The Piggery are beginning to do, in addition to providing delicious food, is erase the lines our industrial society has attempted to draw between human culture and the natural world. The type of practices The Piggery supports do not easily fall into preconceived notions of what is "natural" or "unnatural."

I realize this is a theme that keeps getting revisited here, and especially in this chapter, as I'd like to draw our attention to the sometimes complicated issue of the relationships between humans and the animals we consume. If it isn't obvious, I'd like to brainstorm what such a relationship could look like if not based upon a foundation of abuse. If we care about animals and sustainability and want to eat meat, it is imperative that we deal with these issues. It is imperative that we follow in the footsteps of those that made no such distinction between the natural world and human endeavors.

***

I've heard the argument too many times to not address it preemptively here. *No, we cannot, nor should not, go back to living in caves.* And even if we could, I wouldn't want to because there would be no Piggery there. Billions of us cannot "go back" to the forests in a physical sense. We cannot live and hunt with the same degree of authenticity and necessity as our ancestors. With the current global population, we would decimate all wildlife populations and in the process destroy ourselves. Although our descendants at some point surely will again, we ourselves will never fully know the satisfaction of the hunting and gathering life and all that it brings.

Hunting is a viable and enriching way to acquire nutrition. But even the most avid hunter or forager in our modern culture only supplements his or her diet with food that has come from the woods. I cringe to say it and don't want to. But yes, it is probably an unfortunate truth that we need some form of agriculture. However, regardless of our temporary need to use agriculture as a crutch to get us by until we come up with something better, we also seriously need to "go back" to healthy psychological and physical nourishment based upon evolutionary truths and do this as soon as possible.

To even argue this notion of "going back" is silly. It is based upon the presumption that our linear definition of history is an accurate way to perceive the world. It is based upon the erroneous idea that our civilization is an advanced, more evolved, and more sophisticated (read: superior) way of life. It is the ultimate apex that *we* have reached, and to which all other cultures are, at various stages, working towards. By this logic, those subsistence strategies and social organizations that came before us, are an earlier, primitive, less developed (read: inferior) way of life. This is the assumption of the person who suggests that we cannot go back to living in caves, regardless of their intentions. But how do we go back to something that is impossible for us to have ever left?

The relevant question is not about going back, but rather, what are we going to do *as we move* into the future? What are we to do concerning meat considering that we live in the twenty-first century in an overpopulated world that has been irreversibly altered? I argue we still need to reacquaint our bodies and spirits, on some level, with our non-agricultural heritage. Each step away from domestication, even if not a total abandonment, brings us closer to what it means to be human; towards fulfillment and to a wisdom that can help shine light on our modern dilemmas. And I would argue *because* living "wild" is not a matter of being barbaric and brutish, and living integrated with the land is not a lifestyle below *or* behind us, we don't have to live in caves to do it.

For thousands of years, there has been a widely accepted cultural value ingrained in nearly all of us that a separation exists between what is domesticated and what is wild. I, myself, am guilty of such laziness. In this book, I make the distinction 157 times. I've done it as recently as the previous paragraph and I'll do it again. But do these terms actually have any substantial meaning when it comes down to it?

This distinction has its roots in an age-old anthropological debate concerning what is known as the nature-culture dichotomy. This alleged nature-culture divide is an important value in Western society. It is a concept that has been central to our civilization's ability to attain an unprecedented level of materialist progress and achieve full-fledged economic and cultural globalization. Most people of our culture cling to this dualistic thinking, as it on the surface supports our lifestyle – a lifestyle that most associate with wealth, prosperity, and personal freedom that would not be possible if people did not view the natural world as beneath our supposed "right" to progress. In short, this notion of a nature-culture dichotomy is good for agriculture, technology, and industry.

But as far as the nature-culture divide being an accurate or good way to conceptualize humans in their environment, it would have to hold true that civilization itself is healthy for humans. I have already made the case that there is overwhelming evidence to suggest that it is not – that our culture is a failure of a social arrangement for humans and contradicts our very evolutionary biology as a species. However, what I consider to be the fact that *our* culture stands in conflict with the natural world (insofar as its ability to be sustained) is not to be mistaken for culture *itself* being in conflict with the natural world.

The nature-culture dichotomy is an inadequate, actually *dangerous*, way to conceptualize humans and their environment. In agreement with native wisdom throughout the ages and still today, I reject the nature-culture divide. I reject the idea that culture necessarily degrades nature. In fact, even according to the modern sciences, no such separation exists. I would even argue that there is no real nature-culture divide characterizing our own industrial culture; such a separation is a figment of our collective imagination. As destructive as our civilization is to the environment, even *it* exists in balance with the natural world; eventually it will be eliminated in a very normal way in accordance with ecological laws that keep all else in balance.

Beavers are notorious for altering the environment, yet we don't say there is a nature-beaver dichotomy. Birds and other mammals do as well, but there is not a debate in ornithology whether there is a nature-bird divide. The question is not whether there is a distinction between humans and the rest of the natural world – there isn't. The question should be concerned with how workable a given culture's methods of making a living happen to be and the impact generated. In fact, humans cannot live or create culture separately from the natural world, regardless of how we perceive ourselves in an imagined hierarchy of living things.

So really, though I use the words, for lack of better ones, to illustrate a point, one would be hard pressed to actually define the difference between what is wild and what is domesticated. Is the white-tailed deer that eats daily from a field of genetically modified soybeans really wild? What about the squirrel that eats all my peaches from the human grafted tree that was shipped to me via the United States postal service? And the wolves that can't help but eat domesticated livestock? These are all clear-cut cases where the lines between wildness and domestication aren't clear-cut at all. In fact, they're pretty damn blurry from where I stand.

Which in a way is the silver lining in this screwed up world.

We don't *have* to go back to persistence hunting in our loincloths. We humans can't be prevented from small-scale food production, just as much as we can't prevent the coyote from eating your domesticated kitten if it gets the chance. As much as hunting for our meat is an undeniable product of our evolutionary history, so is opportunity and adaptation. Cultivating food, be it plant or animal, is not evil or unnatural in and of itself. If we choose to, we can approach food production in a non-civilized way.

I can't help but think of wild and domesticated as two poles on a continuum of ecological health. Maybe, the place that we need to approach meat from is some blurry place where wild and domestic meet on that spectrum.

***

Ecology and culture are integrated very intimately in a beautiful dance called adaptation. While foraging, including hunting, is the principal means by which the human animal provides subsistence to their communities, it is not the only means. This is because, like all living components, humans have a dynamic relationship with our environment. Because of our brain size and a host of other physical adaptations, we are enabled to be creative and adapt to an uncanny range of differing habitats. It is more "natural" for humans to alter their habitat based on the needs and preferences of the community than to hunt or gather from some so-called undisturbed, virgin ecosystem. Humans have always had a role in the environment, whether it be burning vast areas to promote biodiversity or the growth of preferred species, shifting cultivation, or simply carrying around a bag of root vegetables and planting them while they squat to poop.

These types of activities fall under the category of horticulture, which is an altogether contrasting strategy from agriculture, in both scale and impact. Non-industrial horticultural food cultivation has been practiced by countless societies successfully throughout human history. These styles of growing food *mimic the diversity of the surrounding ecosystem*, rather than subduing it. They are ecologically sound, and in some cases, rather sophisticated. It is important to understand that horticultural subsistence strategies are in no way a precursor to, or a primitive form of, agriculture.

The Tsembaga people of Paupa New Guinea clear vegetation in the forest in favor of shifting plots of intercropped gardens that produce dozens of species of edible plants. They also raise pigs that keep villages free of garbage and human feces. The Hanunoo of what is now the Philippines likewise have a sophisticated method of companion planting which involves various edible plants species as well as pigs and chickens. The Kuikuru of the South

American tropical forests engage in horticultural practices that even feed large, permanent settlements without destroying the surrounding ecosystems. I could go on and on. In any of these examples, a stranger such as you or I might be hard pressed to figure out where the forest ends and gardens belonging to these cultures begin. Now admittedly, I don't know the workings of these cultures enough to say we should emulate them. However, it is safe to say that their style of food cultivation is very different from what is happening on the farms of our culture to say the least.

And while all of the aforementioned cultures are making a living in ecosystems unfamiliar to most of us, there are also examples from environments closer to home. Where I live, the native people that lived here were the Haudenosaunee, or Iroquois. I am particularly interested in the Iroquois model of food production, not only because of their presence in my bioregion, but because at the time of European invasion, the Iroquois had one foot in civilization and one outside of it. Like ours, their lifestyle was not a reflection of our Paleolithic ancestors, meaning they were not an immediate-return foraging society. They were an agricultural society, and a political and military force to be reckoned with. But they had not yet crossed the line to being a full-scale civilization either. The methods by which they farmed revolved around transplanting perennials in the vicinity of their villages and having them naturalize, in combination with semi-permanent fields consisting of annual polyculture guilds of corn, beans, and squash. They were farmers in some sense of the word, but farmers that respected the land they farmed.

The specifics of what food crops any of these land-based societies raised, or the biomes in which they lived, are not as important as the perspective. What I aim to show is that horticultural societies have come up with adaptive strategies that pretty much defy the standard narrative of agriculturists and environmentalists alike. Such an approach to growing food could be of great value to us today whether being applied to raising plants or animals.

Horticulture is still an ecologically viable form of food production. It offers a high flexibility between cultivated and wild food sources, therefore increasing the potential for a healthy, balanced diet. These traditional methods tend to be highly efficient, productive, and stable. Tools used in horticultural systems are simple, yet very effective. Hoes and digging sticks can be fashioned from natural materials, as opposed to complex machines being assembled by a fossil fueled industrial system. In fact there is no intensive use of factors of production – be it land, labor, capital, or machinery. Horticulture supplements hunting and gathering rather than replacing it. But perhaps most importantly of all, the use of horticultural land plots is not continuous over time, which has far reaching implications.

In non-agricultural cultures characterized by this style of food production, the relationship between people and the land is not static or permanent, so cultivated land can easily recover. Nature isn't beat into submission. The soil is not destroyed. Interference is low-intensity and easily recoverable – the forest grows healthy again. In fact, in most of these cases of human-induced disturbance, biodiversity is actually increased and the removal of humans would have an actual detrimental effect to the ecosystem.

Throw your concept of wilderness out to the compost pile.

***

I know there's a saying that goes something along the lines of "never let them see you sweat." A person providing entertainment, information, or some other service should come off as confident, even if they don't feel it. You can't see me sweat, and luckily you cannot *smell* me sweat, but at this point – though however unprofessional – I will admit this is a challenging chapter to write.

First of all, I had to write about The Piggery with no Texas Hot in my belly. That was difficult enough. But other than that, justifying hunting is easy. Even in the type of horticultural societies mentioned above, hunting is the predominant way humans get meat. And herding has little to offer us in the twenty-first century.

Though many cultures labeled "hunter-gatherers" weren't necessarily strictly so, it is also true that land-based cultures don't often domesticate animals for meat. Rather, they simply alter the environment in ways that produce bumper crops of the native animals they like to eat, and then they hunt them. So basically, if we lived in a world with one million people, I would most certainly make the case that hunting is where we should get all of our meat.

But unfortunately, the world is much more populated and complicated now. Now, we are talking about approaching meat from "some blurry place where wild and domestic meet on the spectrum." Like it or not, we are living in a global economy, and because of that, nothing is manageable as it would be otherwise. We can no longer burn the landscape to provide ideal habitat for elk or carefully place snares on the travel routes of deer. There are no native lands to manage anymore for our communities, just private or government owned so-called property. I don't think the neighbor would appreciate me setting up a deadfall trap in their backyard. I don't think the town would permit deer drives consisting of hundreds of men with spears.

Just as I've attempted to make the case that no nature-culture dichotomy exists, I likewise question whether a native/non-native dichotomy exists anymore, if it ever has. Yup, these are complex issues. When it comes with how to live in balance with the land, I obviously find it necessary to research about the original tribes that inhabited my bioregion. But I also find value in looking to land-based cultures around the globe. I find value in working with regionally specific plants and animals when it comes to sustainable food production, but I am willing to plant non-native perennial vegetables in my garden as an ecologically responsible horticultural practice.

Despite superficial customs and such, there is virtually no cultural diversity in modern society as far as subsistence strategies are concerned. From the West to the East, we work to make money to buy food from agriculturists. Those of us who want an alternative are left working to piece together what a sustainable economy might look like. I am slightly reassured when I see the mind-boggling examples throughout human evolution of our propensity to adapt to environmental conditions. And although animal domestication has never been common among land-based populations, a host of horticultural practices involving plants *have* been. And as intelligent beings, I see no reason to not apply those practices to how we raise animals for food.

In other words, for a variety of complex reasons, we may need to look to other projects in other parts of the world for ideas that could be adapted to work in our specific bioregions.

So despite my admission that I find this chapter more challenging to write than previous ones, I find some relief mixing up some of these theoretical arguments with *examples* of people who are simply engaging in the type of food production I'm advocating. What matters to me most are the hunting strategies and associated rituals of the Cayuga tribe living on this land before European contact. But so do the techniques of 70-year-old Austrian mountain farmers who have been threatened with arrest for maintaining wild forest gardens.

***

I'm guessing you've heard of Joel Salatin and Polyface Farm of *Omnivore's Dilemma* and *Food, Inc.* fame. I appreciate Mr. Salatin's philosophies about farming and his voice in the debate concerning food issues, and you should too. If I lived anywhere near Swoope, Virginia, wherever that is, I would no doubt patronize his farm. Even more likely, I'd ask to hunt his land during deer season. Either way, I appreciate the work the Joel Salatins of the world are doing. But I'd much rather talk about Sepp Holzer. Because while Polyface Farm looks like, well, a *farm* – Sepp Holzer's 100 acres of edible plants and animals looks like a forest, interspersed with pond gardens and flowing terraces. While Joel Salatin supplements his animals' diets with food grown elsewhere, Sepp Holzer's animals are wild fed. Both places produce livestock raised in healthy, holistic ways and should be acknowledged as viable alternatives to conventional, even organic, meat. But Mr. Holzer's methods are about the most ideal and beautiful ways to acquire meat that I have discovered thus far, aside from traditional hunting. And if we are to emulate or learn from others engaged in sustainable animal husbandry, we might as well turn to the most consistent.

So what is it that Sepp Holzer does with his livestock that is so unique? In order to appreciate his methods, it's easier to answer that question with what he *doesn't* do. He doesn't confine them or even lock them up for the night. He barely feeds them if he does at all. No dehorning. No debeaking. No chemicals. No cages. No barns. He doesn't clean after them.

Sepp Holzer's farm, called the Krameterhof, is located in the frigid, harsh mountains of Austria. He's written a couple of books, has been the subject of a couple low budget DVD's, and has some random videos online, but hasn't nearly achieved the notoriety of such farmers as Joel Salatin, and I can't help but wonder why. The only thing I can come up with is that he has no time for fame and interviews because he's too busy spending his days being awesome. Like many of the horticultural cultures mentioned above, Mr. Holzer defies all of our conventional notions of what farming is. The reason is simple. He spends more time observing nature than he does farming. He knows his place, he listens to the land. He questions convention and rejects methods that are not compatible with his land base, even if it means being fined or threatened with prison.

The guy even has a section in one of his books called "Dealing with the Authorities." You don't see that every day in gardening books, and when you do, you know the guy's the real deal. When people gave him the nickname "the rebel farmer," it wasn't lip service or a clever marketing slogan.

I don't even know if anyone, even Sepp Holzer himself, has figured a number of edible or medicinal plants, fungi, or animal species raised on the roughly

100 acres of steep alpine terrain that make up the Krameterhof. Between the fishing ponds, fruit tree forests, nuts, shrubs, vines, vegetables, herbs, mushrooms, animals roaming around free – the number must be staggering compared to what we think can be grown on that same amount of land. Especially for a landscape so rocky and cold. While the Krameterhof is surrounded by fir tree monocultures for miles and miles, the land that farmer Holzer and his wife tend to is teeming with life. But for our purposes here, we're going to focus in on those animals roaming around.

And as you're reading these words, imagining those free roaming animals, don't think of your typical dull overbred pig and cow you've seen on television commercials and covers of picture books. Don't think Wilbur – think Mangalitza wooly pigs. Don't think Clarabelle – think bison, water buffalo, and yaks. Think mouflon and ibexes. Quail. Pheasants. Ducks. Geese. And don't be afraid to take a break from reading this and go look up some images of what an ibex looks like.

Pretty awesome, right?

According to Sepp Holzer, the older the breed, the better adapted it is to be raised in as "wild" a manner as possible. These are hardy animals, suited to the terrain, and I can only assume are happy as hell. And when it comes to sentient creatures that can feel pain, distress, psychological damage, etc., it seems like a pretty damn good philosophy to me.

These animals are kept outside, all year long, living as families or herds in the fresh air as they are meant to. A paddock system is used, whereby groups of animals are rotated to different parts of the landscape, where they loosen soils, consume pests and weeds, till, scatter seeds and spread perennial tubers. They work the land while fulfilling their natural requirements, reducing the need for human labor. However, these aren't draft animals or beasts of burden being exploited. These are pigs being pigs. Chickens being chickens. Ibexes being ibexes.

The paddocks have plenty of space, but not wide-open pasture. There are places to hide from humans and each other if desired. There is a wide variety of natural vegetation ensuring that extra feeding is rarely necessary. They are left alone with their instincts, to determine what and how much to eat. With the exception of the deep, frigid winter, these animals work on their own to get their food.

Disturbance of all kinds is limited, even when it comes to the animals' shelters. One of the practices Sepp Holzer is known for is his use of earth shelters, rather than building barns, on the Krameterhof. Formed with large boulders or tree trunks for walls and built into terraces, they are dry and insulated all throughout the year. Yes, they look very cool, which is probably not insignificant when it comes to their notoriety. But, they are much more than that. They are a reflection of his philosophies about raising food and providing adequate habitat for livestock. Aside from hunting, this is about as diametrically opposed to the factory farming model of animal agriculture as one can get.

So have I answered the question of what makes Sepp Holzer and his livestock raising methods (if that's what they can even be called) so special? If not, I can summarize it now in one sentence.

The animals on the Krameterhof don't need him.

The Highland cow traversing the alpine terrain of the Krameterhof acts as a part of the wild landscape, in the same way that a cassava shrub does in a swidden garden in the middle of the Amazon rainforest. Mr. Holzer himself has said that the focus is not on high yields, but rather the happiness of the animal. He deliberately wants them to retain, what he calls, their wild character. And he accomplishes this by studying their habits and making the appropriate accommodations. These animals are about as free as "livestock" can get. I love it.

When considering and throwing around catch phrases such as "alternative agriculture," it makes industrial organic farming almost seem laughable.

***

Have you ever been asked upon meeting someone new, "So … what do you do?"

I know that you have, and I also know you've asked the question. We all understand that in the context of modern life in the Western world, the meaning of the question is universal. It doesn't actually mean "what do you do?" No one is looking for an answer such as "I contemplate the oak tree in my backyard," or "I play Pictionary with my kids," or "I go to swing dance lessons on Thursday evenings" or "I eat at The Piggery." They don't want to know your passions, your questions, or your observations. They want to know to whom you trade 40 hours or more per week for a paycheck.

This sort of division of labor – the "occupations" we so often ask each other about for some stupid reason – is an invention of agriculture. Civilized people need to be assigned a specific, repetitive task in order to achieve an efficiency that will lead to growth in profit. We all too often act, and are treated, like machines. Land-based people certainly may have roles to play in their community. They certainly have sophisticated skills. But they just aren't specialized in the same way. They aren't domesticated. There's that word again. Let's rephrase and say it this way: they aren't broken.

If one had to assign a title or profession to a typical member of a land-based community that was the equivalent of a modern profession, what could that be? There are no marketing careers, no IT jobs, no aerospace engineers, no secretaries, tractor trailer drivers, or waitresses. There may be a healer, a chief or a storyteller – but I'm talking about a typical member. I came up with only three careers that could be assigned to just about anyone to describe the work they do. The first is that of a craftsman or craftswoman (or craftspersyn if you're an ecofeminist). The second is that of a naturalist. Really, these are both the same and I already discussed the concept of traditional ecological knowledge as universal in non-agricultural societies. The third is an ecological designer. There you have it, three modern names for ancient professions that could very well hold some clues to the question of how we could acquire meat while not supporting factory farming.

What do I mean by ecological design?

What I mean has nothing to do with some omnipotent creator. There is no single solitary attribute that fundamentally separates humans from any other mammal. But we do (sometimes) have a more developed ability to reason and create culture. On a superficial level, this seems like both a blessing and a curse, doesn't it? The point though, is that we *design* more than other species. It's not that other species don't design, but because of our brain size, we alone have the ability – thus, choice – to design in ways that do not really flow with the order of life. For the great majority of our existence, we designed tools, villages, art, clothing, gardens, etc. in the same harmonious manner weaverbirds make intricate and elegant nests. But the last several thousand years has proven how far astray our design skills have wandered.

Humans design. Like we tell stories. Like we play. It's part of our genetic makeup. For hundreds of thousands of years, we were ecological designers. In the past couple of decades, a new field has emerged where people take classes, get degrees, and get paid for ecological design. Of course, this so-called "new" cutting edge system of knowledge (uggh) is largely being applied to manufacturing industries and technology. In other words, we are supposedly ecologically designing things we want to consume. But I personally see much less ecological design of things we actually *need*. Like shelter, water, health care, systems for bearing and raising children, and nutrition – including meat.

It seems on the surface that the concepts of raising food animals and re-establishing productive and diverse grasslands, woodlands, etc. are incompatible. If I have not made the case yet, I will blatantly say here that I am not so convinced. Although I am not one of those well-paid ecological designers and certainly not a representative of any tribal land-based culture well accomplished in these matters, I do happen to notice a few things.

I *do* know that as a member of the Northern hardwood forest community, I have a great respect for forest ecosystems. I also know that conventional animal agriculture is at odds with the living community I call home, as agriculture as we know it necessarily *destroys* forest ecosystems. I know that no ecosystem is composed of isolated, incomplete pieces. No living thing serves only one function. The living world is layered and vigorous, and its components are interrelated in a myriad of complex ways, many of which we don't even understand. No strategic approach from any animal attempting to acquire any resource can succeed independently from the ecology of a place.

In a bioregional future, humans will need to be close to all their necessary resources, which means forest *and* food. The line that western culture drew attempting to divide nature and culture will have to be erased. I imagine a mosaic of ecosystems, but not fractured and fenced like we might see in rural areas today. As opportunists, we eat from multiple biological kingdoms. We need to conserve natural communities and raise our food with a recognition and respect for how they all operate on a physical and energetic level.

What I know when it comes to raising meat is that animals and plants and fungus and all that other tasty stuff out there operates together all across the world – on every biome on every continent. We need more and more and more and more people to become naturalists and ecological designers. With more people refusing to bow down to the fallacy of the nature-culture dichotomy, and more familiarity about the workings of the natural world – which includes *us* – we may begin to come up with more bioregional solutions to our food issues.

So … what do *you* do?

***

The Piggery, Sepp Holzer … this chapter didn't end up being so bad after all. It is obvious that human ingenuity is an adaptation that can be used to serve a community, which I say is synonymous with serving the land. Or, it can be misused to serve short-term profit margins and convenience. We obviously have examples of both. What most modern people fail to realize, however, is that while human ingenuity is an amazing characteristic of our species, it is not at all above or separate at all from the laws that govern the natural world. I've already given due credit for our abilities to reason, think, and invent. But these abilities do not make civilization special, or even good. Bats can use echolocation to navigate for food. The wing feathers of barn owls reduce noise caused by turbulence so they fly silently and undetected by prey. All predators are equipped with adaptations to make the acquisition of meals efficient. Some have keen eyesight or hearing. Humans evolved with an intelligence that a large percentage of us have been misusing for the better part of 10,000 years.

When we decide to use that ingenuity for something other than accumulating so-called wealth, causing selfish destruction of our surroundings, beautiful things can happen. We are a clever and creative species thanks to our history as hunters. We can use this brainpower to learn from both inspirational horticultural societies of the past *and* present, as well as the contemporary sustenance farmers that are innovative, creating fresh methods of raising food based on time-tested ancestral knowledge. Land-based people are keen when it comes to growing or foraging food. While we complacently consume food, they are actively engaged with their food. We have the examples of those committed to bioregional principles of sustainability and food security. We have access to all of it. But first, we need to move forward into the future with the unconventional realization that the nature-culture dichotomy is a fallacy, as are all environmental dogmas that dictate that we should be leaving nature alone.

On one end of the ecological health spectrum, there is sustainably hunting for the meat one's family will eat. And on the other, there is controlling the lives of sentient livestock species in every cruel and conceivable way possible in order minimize costs and maximize profits. Modern animal agriculture operates without restraint, viewing animals as property, as inanimate parts on an assembly line. Western civilization thrives on domestication, a process of control, a process for which we are paying a severe price. This is extremism in every sense of the word. The absurdity is that we have created something that will destroy us. There are undeniably other ways and always have been. We need to eat, but animals are not commodities.

We could stand to scoot over a little bit on that spectrum.

We are not the Mekranoti or the Yanomami who are adept at cultivating food without depleting their land base. We are mostly a bunch of incompetent boneheads that might look spiffy, but are usually blind, deaf and dumb when it comes to anything of real value. However the truth is, when it comes down to it, we *do* have the same brain capacity as members of any other society. Even the ones with beautiful forest gardens, life-affirming rituals, skills, craftsmanship and wisdom so far above and beyond that of the civilized world. We are all *Homo sapiens* and evolved with the same human genes. The same basic human ingenuity.

Forget politicians or sustainable development or global environmentalism. Forget the "What Would Jesus Do?" bumper stickers. When it comes to food, I want a "What would Sepp Holzer do?" sticker. I want a "I got porked at The Piggery" sticker instead of a "Got milk?" sticker.

"I break for ibexes?" "Honk if you love swidden farmers?"

Non-civilized humans have always manipulated the environment in ecologically viable ways to produce favored foods. Today, a small but growing handful of folks in our very own culture are figuring out ways to do the same. It follows that we *can* raise meat based on similar principles. We *can* preserve forests while eating steak for dinner.

What we need are more visionaries. What we desperately need are new stories.

Maybe what we need even more at this point is a path to *healing*, so that more of us can arrive at a state of well-being that leaves us better equipped to write those new stories.

7. RECOVERY

"It is no measure of health to be well adjusted to a profoundly sick society."

Jiddu Krishnamurti

Healing takes many forms.

And though they are inextricably intertwined, there exist several areas on which one could potentially focus healing strategies: our suffering minds, our sick bodies, or our debilitated environments, to name a few. Unfortunately for us all, we live in a world of collective disease. There are countless antidotes that are possible which have been handed to us by the pharmaceutical industries, psychologists, shamans and poets alike. Fortunately for my argument, it just so happens that the methods by which we can reclaim the acquisition of meat are incredibly therapeutic on a variety of levels. As much as this book is about meat, or respecting tribal cultures, or ex-vegan deer slayers – this book is about holistic medicine. Not the kind of holistic medicine that looks like homeopathy or reiki or acupuncture. But the kind of holistic medicine that looks like *getting the hell outside* and interacting with the animals and land around you. Because when we do, we will find symptoms of all sorts of nasty afflictions begin to alleviate.

Sustenance hunting and raising livestock are no longer all-American traditions for white, rural Bible thumpers. In the context of the world we live in, hunting and humanely raising meat animals is actually nothing short of subversive to the status quo. Western civilization, and the institutions that uphold it, survive by making us reliant on them. Agribusiness is driven by profit, nothing else. Because I haven't said it in a few pages, I'll get back on my locally and sustainably harvested wooden soapbox for a moment and have the audacity to say they do not care about your health, or the health of the environment. And in fact, industrial agriculture has ravaged both, to the point that only degraded shadows of what once was remain.

We are a weakened species, barely surviving in weakened habitats. Sedentary lives lived driving and texting across a wasteland. Given this, any attempt to take our lives back into our own hands or that of our community is a revolutionary act. More accurately, it is an act of *rehabilitation*. Reclaiming the means to acquire our own meat is not only an alternative to the factory farming system, it is a means to provide nutrients to our family and a boon to our psychological well being. On top of this, these methods can be rejuvenating to the land. The fact that the thought of hunting or otherwise killing animals makes most civilized people uncomfortable is a possible indicator that it has health benefits – in the same way bitter greens are detoxifying to our body. Sometimes we're just not in tune with those things that are good for us.

This may not be intuitive for most of us who were born and bred within our culture and are very much used to our dirty work happening for us, elsewhere. People fear what they don't understand and make a moral judgment accordingly. Crazy shamans. Country bumpkins. Dirty hippies. Ignorant rednecks. Wicked witches. Our society ostracizes all that is close with the land, be it a farmer or a snake. We humans are above the slimy, slithery, mucky things that live in "the wild" after all. We were meant for greater things than frogs and worms and cavemen. (Like diabetes, online porn, and remote keyless car starters.)

So it is that living "close to nature" is seen as synonymous to living in a way that is foul. Children cannot even play outdoors anymore lest they get muddy. Sometimes, playing in the soil is cause for actual punishment. For these reasons, any action that requires an immersion in the natural world is restorative for a populace that knows little else other than the synthetic and sanitized. If encouraging our kids to simply play outdoors has been shown to alleviate the symptoms of Nature Deficit Disorder, then inspiring them by example to forage, hunt, and help with small-scale animal husbandry could have impacts beyond our ability to predict.

Over and over since my ex-career as an herbivore – and still in recent times – I've heard this fallacy that meat is damaging to one's health. It's hard to digest. It's toxic to our system. Saturated fat and cholesterol. Blah, blah, blah. I tell you from being on both sides of this dietary debate … it's propaganda. Industrial food propaganda adopted by, and subsequently used as, vegetarian propaganda. It's time to leave that junk corn oil on the grocery store shelf and pick up a good ole fashioned tub of artery-clogging lard from the farm on your way home. It may go against conventional advice, but don't be surprised, like I was, how much better off you'll be.

***

I did try in earnest to not get into nutrition in this book. This chapter, however, is about health, and so forgive me if a couple things I mention here get a little too close for comfort to that obnoxious topic. Feel free to skip this section altogether … heck, I would. But for the rest of you who aren't going to skip ahead (It's okay, I won't be offended), let me ask you a question.

What do you think is going to happen to your personal health, when the food you put in your mouth is totally out of accordance with the way your species has evolved for hundreds of thousands of years?

Is it possible to discuss subjects such as those that I'm broaching without getting into the field of nutritional science? As far as our modern sciences go, anthropology is intriguing to me. I can tolerate ecology so long as it doesn't get too technical. But I really don't like nutrition. What are antioxidants anyways? What is glycemic load? Lipids? Can you articulate what a protein actually is? Can *anyone*? Well, whether we are a clearinghouse of useless nutritional terminology or not, we all need to eat, now don't we? I don't know. Our hominid ancestors didn't have master's degrees in clinical nutrition or food technology back in the day, yet somehow without the benefit of modern nutritional science, they got by. They probably ate too … and obviously did so healthily enough to propagate the species without destroying the earth.

So I'm not going to talk about Vitamin B-12. I'm not going to discuss Omega 3's. Amino acids? Not even iron? Nope. Not gonna do it. Because I don't want to and it's my book dammit. Maple pork rinds from The Piggery? Maybe.

The reality is, this kind of reductionist science is confusing to most people, especially when it comes to food, which is a topic quite close to most peoples' hearts.

What is important to our recovery is that anthropologists and the like who study such things have discovered that pre-agricultural humans (as well as many present-day indigenous populations) were more fit, had denser bones and had better teeth than modern man. Not only were they physically more robust, but they also had little in the way of infectious diseases. Cancer, diabetes, and other chronic illnesses were foreign, if not nonexistent. They were (and are) healthier than us civilized folks and the reasons are simple. One being that their diet was/is composed of fresh, whole, nutrient dense foods, including a proper balance – according to bioregion – of plant and *animal* material.

We have the stamina to potentially run long distances. We have the brains to develop tools and work together to catch food. We have senses adequate to stalk and find it. Our digestive tract is quite an extraordinary system with capabilities to process a wide variety of plants and animals. We are opportunists *in too many ways to dispute the point*. Like it or not, regardless of philosophical differences, we are genetically designed to consume at the very least a small proportion of meat, and in all likelihood, more than that. Moreover, hunting and fishing as a means to acquire food is an inseparable part of our evolutionary history. Such practices have a long and universal character for bioregional cultures, especially when compared to our short time as agriculturists. The differences we see in diets between land-based cultures have everything to do with climate and what is available. Not between herbivory and carnivory.

Sure, we *can* live sedentary lives behind a screen eating crap, but inside, our genes are still that of a hunter-gatherer. This is a fact to be acknowledged if we intend to thrive rather than merely survive. It just so happens that even still in the twenty-first century, wild meat – and meat likewise raised in natural conditions – is hands down, some of the most nutritional foods you can put into your body.

If any self-proclaimed expert attempts to tell you about a magical diet or the "secret" to good health, they probably have ulterior motives. This isn't rocket science. Sure, there are those out there that make it complicated and intimidating because there is a disgusting amount of profit to be made off of sick people. There's no shortage of overweight people who have money. No shortage of folks suffering from diabetes and heart disease that have money. But here it is; I'll save you a few bucks.

We, as primates, are designed to eat plants *and* animals and should do so with a holistic approach. Weird things like offal, fermented vegetables, saturated fat, and chocolate are probably good for you. We are not designed to over-consume grains, sugar (unless combined with chocolate) or refined carbohydrates in general. The decline of public health testifies to this fact, and one doesn't need to be a biochemist or a low-carb disciple to see the evidence. I still find the consumption of another animal's milk unjustifiably unnatural as indicated by the fact that no other animal steals and consumes another species' baby's milk. Not that there aren't more pressing food matters to attend to, so if raw milk and kefir is your thing, knock yourself out. But eating factory farmed meat is physical and spiritual poison and not so easily exonerated.

That's my one paragraph of dietary recommendations.

I simply contend that one simply embrace simplicity when it comes to diet. *Simple*, right? Then why the hell does everyone need to make it so complicated? The food we eat should be diverse, nutrient dense, clean, holistic, and above else sustainable.

And by now, you know that when I say sustainable, I mean food grown bioregionally whenever possible.

Wellness is not a one-way street. You can't just hope your way to being healthy. It's an interactive process, and I'll keep hammering this point throughout the chapter because I went ahead and called it "Recovery." If you interact with the outside world in a healthy way, you will receive mental benefits. If you interact with the land and what it provides in a healthy way, the land will be enriched. If you interact with your food (which is simply one embodiment of the land) in a healthy way, your physical body will be stronger.

I might be a techno-dunce, but I'm still living in the twenty-first century. I occasionally read blogs and check out websites when I should be reading the landscape or checking out tracks. And as antisocial as I unfortunately can be, I still talk to people. I have discovered that there is a surprisingly large population of vegetarians who have suffered similar symptoms as I have. I'm no super athlete. My body fat percentage is probably not exactly what I'd prefer it to be. But having since started incorporating nutritious meat into my diet, I've lost 30 pounds, ran a barefoot half marathon, earned a black belt in Aikido, and am in better shape overall than all my previous adult years as a vegetarian. Now, if I could just lay off the non-dairy coconut milk ice cream....

Based on personal experience, the human story, as well as modern research, I can unequivocally say that wild meat is physically healthy. But the acquisition of that meat, when done from a conscientious perspective involving bioregional methods and techniques, is perhaps a much bigger favor to our health in ways beyond physical nutrition.

***

What about psychological healing? While trying to be as sensitive as possible, I will admit there is no shortage of mental imbalance around me, as I'm sure it is the case with you. It's everywhere. Like the rampant, vicious plagues of past eras, only more insidious because now our nuclear families hide behind our closed suburban doors with no one to bear witness to our shortcomings, while before people suffered in the open. Today, there is no accountability. No support other than that which can be bought for a high price. Silent mental suffering is the pandemic of our generation.

My sister died as an adult from such mental illness. I, myself, struggle plenty – no thanks to civilization. It's challenging to keep perspective with so much out there to trigger anger, anxiety, sadness, and insecurity. Often it's hard to muster fortitude when abuse is so habitual and encompassing of our culture. Sometimes, I've wondered how I cope, why I did not end up like my sister. And one of the only things I can think of that differentiates me is that I made a choice that embraced life as a teenager, and that evolved into an affinity for the natural world, my source of vitality.

Sometimes, communing with the untamed is my only source of comfort.

Just in the past week of writing this paragraph, I was having a conflict with my wife right before I was leaving to hunt for a bit before the sun went down. I left furious and anxious. I went back to the woods, sat back against a tree, tuned in to the environment around me, and felt the fresh autumn breeze against my face. It was soothing and peaceful and offered a clear perspective that allowed me to return a while later to turn things around.

No, I don't always do this. But just imagine if this could happen more frequently with more of us on a grander scale.

Is meat going to save us? No, but it certainly may be part of the wellness equation.

**

Why, you might be asking, does a discussion about psychological health even belong in a book about meat? Doesn't it make more sense to talk about how grass-fed beef contains uncanny amounts of beneficial omega-3 fats? The short answer is because natural processes are all interconnected – especially when it comes to matters of health. And this isn't nearly as talked about as other aspects of human health. Once again, the better answer lies, of course, in how our species evolved. It is very much relevant, if not integral, when discussing human psychological dysfunction that we simultaneously look at human evolution. And when we do that, we are led to the following crucial point.

One indication of our level of detachment from the living world is the major shortage of sensual activity in our lives. We live in a sense-deprived environment compared to land-based populations, where sensual experience is extensive, rich, and whole. We, on the other hand, have machines and computers to regulate our lives, and what cannot be accomplished by non-living technology we usually outsource to someone else. Our dwellings, where we spend most of our time – including our work places and vehicles – are often ugly and climate controlled. Cultural norms insist that we are only allowed to physically touch one person passionately until death do us part. And often, we are usually to fatigued, bored or detached to even with them. Our visual stimulation predominantly comes from screens. Our food is processed and bland. Gosh, no wonder we are depressed!

And to make matters worse, we are becoming increasingly numb with each passing generation. We don't want to be exposed to the elements. We don't even notice the steady hum of insects or the songs of birds all around us, let alone understand them. Our eyesight has deteriorated from lack of use in far or wide-angle vision. Our vision is narrow in a very literal sense, largely because we gave up hunting. At any given time, without our fancy GPS navigation systems, we don't know north from south or notice which way the wind blows.

The absence of predators, as well as the denial of our own role as predators, has been the driving force behind this deterioration. We have neglected our senses to the point that our level of awareness has been reduced to a shadow of what is possible. In fact, if it wasn't for the artificial conveniences offered to us by our cheap energy-fueled economy, our inattentiveness and laziness would likely lead to our very demise as a species.

The historical and anthropological fact is that, by far, the longest of the ecological phases our ancestors lived within was characterized by a hunting and gathering way of life. We have already explored the predominant role hunting has played in our physical and mental development as a species. The implications of this are profound. If it holds true that the bioregional acquisition of meat has sculpted our relationship to the environment, and it also holds true that our mental well-being results, even in part, from the health of that environment, then it must follow that the bioregional acquisition of meat can only benefit our mental well-being.

However, rather than frame it as a math equation, we can simply explore what this relationship looked like for hundreds of thousands of years.

I would think there would be little denial of the assumption that while living as hunter-gatherers, humans were intimately familiar with their environment, a point I've already made. It is obvious that we had to be in order to survive. But we must not neglect the additional fact that *our senses* were (and are) the *means* by which we humans have come to know the environment. Our senses, the ones we know of – sight, sound, smell, taste, and touch – serve our mental health amazingly well, if we only rouse them once in a while.

The environment is alive. It is animate. Some scientists have even come out in support of a theory known as the Gaia hypothesis. The Gaia hypothesis states that the planet, by regulating factors such as its own temperature, the composition of the atmosphere, the salinity of the oceans, etc. acts as if it is a living organism. The earth is literally *alive?* These are not New Age quacks, these are chemists and microbiologists. The field is called geophysiology.

But when I say the environment is alive, that is not what I'm referring to. I find this theory fascinating, even if unsurprising. But I don't believe in Gaia. I do, however, very much believe in the spirit of place.

I'm referring to the vibrant colors and interesting shapes and aesthetic stimuli of all varieties pulsating in the fields and forests around me. I'm referring to the energizing aroma of a stand of conifers, the soothing smell of soil and decomposing straw, and the musky, yet stimulating, odor of deer. I'm referring to the lusciousness of a raspberry as it hits the tongue and the mouthwatering taste of grilled steak. I'm referring to the breeze caressing my face and the cool damp soil between my bare toes. I'm referring to the chorus of bird song, the clucking of chickens, and the crunching of leaves. Who needs Greek goddesses when one can associate with all this beauty?

The prevalence of animistic cosmologies among land-based cultures testifies to the fact that they view their sentient bodies as a mere extension of a sentient world. They do not perceive themselves as an "other." The world – from rocks to mountains to plants and animals – is perceived as literally possessing life. This is because interaction dictates perception. Non-civilized, or place-based humans, use their animal senses habitually, as it is how they sustain themselves. They are attuned to the rhythms and vibrations of their place. Because of this, their sensual experience is rich. Not only this, but there is a layering of sensual experience that is simply not as common among the civilized.

I keep falling into this trap of saying "they" as if "they" are some other species. But I am discussing *human* traits. I'm talking about the awareness that we, as humans, once had. Some still do, and we all *still have* access to it.

Most of us understand that senses are the means by which we understand our surroundings. We know that our senses offer us pleasure and protection. But, in my experience, not many people have considered the role that these experiences have played in shaping the human body and mind. The stimulation of our senses creates chemical and physical changes within us. Through contemplating how our species evolved and how land-based peoples still live, there is a strong case to be made that the psyche is not an individual entity, but one component of a whole eco-logy. We are so estranged from our place in this living system that we are capable of systematically annihil-ating forests, rivers, cultures, and species after species. No living community does this unless they are inflicted with widespread disorder resulting from psychological trauma.

In the 1990's, a clinical psychologist named George Burns developed what he called the sensual awareness inventory. This came to fruition during his "career-long search" for methods of therapy that were the most efficient for providing his clients with actual practical solutions. An observation that Burns had made in his informal relations with other therap-ists is that there was an inconsistency in their prescriptions for their clients and what they them-selves did to attain personal balance in times of difficulty. Many of his colleagues enjoyed outdoor activities such as hiking, gardening, and scuba diving to relax while asking their clients to think, overana-lyze, take drugs, and overanalyze some more. He found that when people are asked to list activities from which they derive pleasure, enjoyment, or com-fort, the majority of those examples are *nature-based activities*. Perhaps needless to say, his techniques were met with great success.

The industrialized world we live in, with its focus on sedentary lifestyles, technology, ownership, and individualism has caused all of these senses to operate in unbalanced ways. Mass production leaves little room for variation. Every loaf of bread tastes the same. Every ear of corn is uniform. Every relationship is a sad carbon copy of the next. Static. Mechanized. It is no wonder, considering how we have evolved as living connected beings, that mental disorders of all kinds are rampant in our culture. Maybe what we need is not anti-depressants and expensive self-help programs. We simply need to be *let out of the damn cage* and enjoy access to a dose of euphoria once in a while. What we need is a prescription for more spontaneity, more wildcrafting and creating, more oral stories, more mischief, more games, more campfires, more dirty feet, more dancing, more sex, and more meat. Scandalous!

Meat. That's what this book is supposedly about. From birth to slaughter to getting swallowed, hunting and/or raising animals and eating them is a positively sensual experience. I have a gut feeling that many, if not most, of the vegetarians out there who were being honest with themselves could not even deny the tantalizing smell of a juicy burger on the grill. The rich taste of properly cooked flesh, oozing with luscious warm fat, tender or chewy, an experience for the mouth. And the variation, even if subtle, offered by naturally raised meat is a thanksgiving in its own right.

Admit it. People crave meat almost as universally as they enjoy a beautiful sunrise. I'm sorry. I didn't make the rules. But it's just not the same way with soymilk or romaine lettuce.

Am I making too great a stretch to claim that eating meat equates to an integration with the universe?

Maybe, maybe not. But is that not the very purpose and result of any sensory experience? The fact is that *any* effort to regain some of the tactile experience that we evolved with is good for mental health.

What this all amounts to is this: A whole new, deep world awaits for those who wish to increase their awareness and practice doing so. The more positively sensual experiences you have, the ones that are in line with the long established human-environment relationship, the happier you're likely to be. Eating meat is one of these experiences. And more so than eating meat, getting that meat on your table is an even *better* way to experience the depth of the natural world.

***

We acknowledge that we live in a time period in which human psychological dysfunction seems to be the norm, rather than the exception. However, there has never been a reason to believe that such widespread stress, anxiety, depression, fear, and a long list of other mental disorders, are a natural part of human existence, prevalent as they may be. It's not just me and my crazy sentiments for land-based cultures. Growing numbers of people over the years have been attributing these types of negative mental conditions to the environment, or rather, our distorted relationship to the environment. Enter "ecopsychology," the banner under which the evolution of the connection between the fields of psychology and ecology could continue.

We've already discussed the problem, but what solutions are being generated by the ecopsychologists? Well, eco*therapy* of course! In summary, ecotherapy is applied ecopsychology. The eco-goal of this eco-movement is to address a root cause of these types of mental disorders and provide eco-tools to restore the fractured relationship most of us have with the environment. (Okay, okay, I'll stop. This is serious stuff.)

There are two points that we can glean from the growing field of ecopsychology. First, the crisis that is our collective lunacy is not simply a biological or ecological one, but fueled by various social and psychological phenomena that have resulted from our civilization's ongoing dissociation with the natural world. Second, there are a variety of antidotes to the mental disorders that result from this dissociation that, in one way or another, discard traditional psychological therapeutic methods in favor of ones that are nature-based. Examples of these could be animal-assisted therapy, horticultural therapy, movement in nature, or dream tending.

All of which, by the way, we will see can be associated with how we put food in our bellies.

Maybe it's wishful thinking, or just the type of people I tend to roll with, but it seems that many people are waking up to the idea that the health of any living system is not dependent on any one factor. In other words, our health is interrelated with countless other ingredients. And so it makes sense that therapy aims for *integration*. Over and over again, research suggests that simply being outdoors has restorative effects on the human psyche. Fatigue, boredom, poor self-esteem and stress all tend to diminish with a mere walk in the woods. The reasoning is because we are engaging our senses in something other than numbing modern technologies. Even a simple walk in the woods or through a creek offers welcome sensory stimulation, beginning to connect us physically, mentally, and emotionally with the land.

So, let me one up the ecotherapists. Instead of just *walking* through the woods, what about consciously attempting to *blend* with those woods as one navigates through them, perhaps, say, on a hunt. If walking outdoors has tangible psychological benefits, what about visualizing that you are actually a *part* of the woods as you do so? Rather than being just a visitor, what could be possible if one were to embrace his or her own nature by considering themselves no different from the owls and fox and bobcats that roam those woods stalking prey? If a tenet of ecotherapy is that we are alienated because we have been uprooted from our environment, why not go back to where we belong, even if only temporarily, as hunters and gatherers?

Another common technique utilized in the field of ecopsychology is animal assisted therapy. The idea behind this technique is that the human-animal bond is profound and timeless. People take walking meditations through a herd of horses. Dogs are brought into mental institutions, improving morale and increasing feelings of calmness for patients. Research shows that retired people who care for pets live longer. Since around the middle of the twentieth century, Americans are spending 90-95% of our time indoors, largely isolated from other living things. This is unprecedented. Having animal companions helps soften the consequences of this insanity.

So let's take these concepts and, once more, one-up the ecotherapists. What if we perceived ourselves, not as owners of animals, but *as* animals ourselves? Rather than viewing non-humans as tools for the treatment of humans, what if we viewed our relation-ship to them as one of reciprocity. Instead of relying on domesticated animals, trained to do as we please, what if we attempted to assist in re-wilding them as much as possible within the periphery of civilization? I've argued that bioregionalism is a form of home-coming, allowing us to live, create, and eat in accordance to place. It follows that we could give pigs, goats, and turkeys a proper homecoming by let-ting them roam in pasture with space and elements, living and eating in accordance to place as well.

We don't belong within civilization, and livestock do not belong in factories. Living off a land base is satisfying and replaces civilized alienation, whether we are a human or a chicken. With the animals we consume living outdoors, we find ourselves outdoors tending to them. All the sights, smells, and feelings that go along with such a lifeway are gifted to us.

Reciprocity. The human-animal bond is fallacy. We *are* animals, and so of course there is a bond with our other relations. When we take responsibility for the meat we eat, we are exposed to those animals. Not cuts of meat, but animals with whom we relate. Our physical functioning improves along with our disposition.

I could go on, because frankly, I'm having fun taking all these ecotherapeutic treatments and correlating them with meat. But you've probably gotten the eco-point by now.

Whether it be horticultural therapy, animal assisted therapy, or any other form of ecotherapy, there are couple of questions that arise. How do we want to spend our time? In front of screens or in the woods? With machines or animals? In a cubicle or in the pasture? When we are choosing how to allocate our valuable time, there is almost always a choice on how we can do so in a manner that is aligned with nature's patterns, therefore supporting our mental stability as well as the stability of the bioregion.

We are deeply scarred and need deep healing, and the root of all this derangement is a dysfunctional way of relating to the world. Land-based, outdoor activities fulfill an emptiness. They remedy illness. Many gardeners, hunters, fishers, farmers, and backpackers experience a calmness when partaking in these activities that is rarely achieved otherwise. They experience an awareness. It is an awareness that results from being present. And awareness is healing.

At home (and I'll trust you know by now what I mean by "home"), we can quiet the clutter of the mind. We can listen to the unnamed, shapeless forces that regulate all the processes of the land. We can remember that we are embodied within an environment of other beings we may no longer understand, but the original human inhabitants surely did. And even if we cannot seem to attain this level of connection (I sure can't most of the time), it simply feels good to feel at ease in a natural environment. Small-scale diverse farms – along with woods, rivers, meadows and other places labeled as "wild" – are truly sacred places that nurture and regenerate. They offer therapy that our churches and hospitals and twelve-step programs could only dream of. They also happen to be the places where we can get dinner from.

As Randall Eaton writes so eloquently in his book *The Sacred Hunt*, "The aboriginal man and woman live within each and every one of us. Their medicine will always be wilderness and the blood and spirit of wild animals." Thanks, Dr. Eaton.

***

Unnamed, shapeless forces? Did I actually just write that a couple paragraphs back? Sometimes, I get in a mode and I don't know where these things come from. It's not that I don't mean this stuff in a very genuine way, its just that being awake at two in morning in front of a glowing monitor isn't "in accordance with the way our species has evolved for hundreds of thousands of years." I should be horizontal in my bed with my windows open, journeying through the dream world, breathing the fresh cool air. Instead, I'm sitting in this stuffy room with glazed eyes behind this godforsaken machine, flirting with delirium. So, let's move on to something more unromantic for the moment, such as how our collective trauma, as I've described above, leads to widespread apathy. And that apathy is causing us to sit back and literally allow the devastation of the natural world to continue in our name. I'm not alluding to the spirit world anymore. I'm talking about the physical world, the one we depend upon in every way.

There is a dead zone in the Gulf of Mexico that is nearly 9,000 square miles, caused by agricultural pollutants being emptied by the Mississippi River. To add insult to injury, *five million barrels* of crude oil recently gushed into the gulf, destroying hundreds of miles of estuaries and wetlands, leaving hundreds of species at risk. In fact, I'm going to shut up about this because the environmental impacts of this oil spill are immeasurable. Another figure that is impossible to measure is rate of species extinction, but scientists try nonetheless using a variety of formulas. Conservative estimates are that about three species go extinct each hour. I won't even scare you with some of the higher numbers. How about a global collapse of fisheries or unprecedented birth defects? Some, for good reason, consider these among the greatest challenges of our time. How can we protect the environment after decades, centuries, of its being ravaged by the civilized world?

Do you remember how I arrogantly simplified the solution to widespread nutritional disorder and the related confusion that results from it, just a little while back? Well, I'm about to suggest just as simple a solution to that whole long scary list of ecological woes we face. Here it is. Gratitude.

It may seem that taking on these global environmental catastrophes of one kind or another is overwhelming. Believe me, I get that. But is it that difficult to look at the land where you are right now, and ask; "What would this place look like if we humans lived here in a way that reflected all that we owe it? How *did* non-civilized people live here before being assimilated or destroyed? What would living bioregionally on *this here land* look like?" It's simple. That doesn't mean applying such a vision is easy, accessible, or even legal.

Fortunately, I have a couple of environmental success stories brought to you, without apology, by the hands of people embracing various aspects of sustainable meat. I've already argued the point that protecting the environment does not equate to leaving it alone. Sometimes, great strides can be made just from making your living in a conscientious way. Like hunting for your food. Oh boy, here I go again.

To the dismay of animal welfare advocates everywhere, who like to hug trees and cute fuzzy animals and cry when they watch Bambi, hunters are responsible for the most substantial conservation efforts in this country since we white folks descended like locusts upon this land. At first, it wasn't pretty. In fact, it was abhorrent, with a holocaust against the people who were living here, rampant deforestation, boundless murder of animals and all. Passenger pigeons, mountain lions, wolves – if a hell exists, surely many a hunter resides there. But since the late nineteenth century, hunter's organizations such as Ducks Unlimited, the Rocky Mountain Elk Foundation, the National Wild Turkey Association and a list of others, have raised millions of dollars, leading directly to major habitat restoration and environmental education.

Yes, like it or not, it is hunters that have had some of the biggest hands in environmental conservation and wildlife programs in the last century. If you hunt in the U.S., you know very well all the license fees and taxes you must pay. First of all, nearly 75 percent of the annual income of state fish and game agencies is paid for out of your pockets. These are the agencies that protect our environment on the state level. On the federal level, there are taxes on archery equipment, all firearms, and ammunition. Billions of dollars have been used to protect forests and wetlands. Now, I'm not one to suggest that money or government will save anything in the longterm absent a new cultural paradigm, but I am suggesting that hunters in this country currently are the primary source of financial support for wildlife and habitat conservation.

What I will also suggest is that if you like to utilize public land to watch birds or hike or walk your dog, or partake in other nature-related recreational activities, perhaps you should realize it is hunters that pay for a large chunk of that state and federal land, not vegetarians. In fact, if hunting were to magically end, then so would the conservation of millions of acres of wild places and those that inhabit them. There would be little stopping developers who would bulldoze these places, one after the other, in the name of suburban sprawl and the so-called American dream. It is no accident that hunters, along with organic farmers, as a whole spend vast amounts of energy and financial resources working and volunteering towards environmental conservation efforts.

Speaking of farmers, let us switch gears for a moment and talk about how environmental conservation and pastured livestock relate.

Ever hear of carbon sequestration? No? Well, you probably have heard that many experts tend to agree that we are living in age of warming climate that has been induced by human activities such as deforestation, burning fossil fuels, and industrial farm animal production. You may have also heard about some of the potential catastrophic consequences of such climate change, or at the very least have seen some apocalyptic disaster movie of one kind or another. Well, one of those greenhouse gases you may have heard of is carbon dioxide. Now, I'm not a chemist, and chances are, you are not either. But from my layperson understanding, carbon sequestration is simply the removal of carbon dioxide from the atmosphere. All in all, not a bad idea, considering. The problem is that some of the proposed methods of doing this are expensive and/or unsafe. But some do have potential, for instance, the preservation of bogs, reforestation, and raising animals on pasture. Hmm.

I mentioned the practice of rotating livestock between paddocks in an earlier chapter as an alternative form of animal agriculture. But because we're talking about healing the environment, let's get into a couple more details concerning the role that could be played in this effort by symbiotic relationships between livestock and the land.

There are several names for it that I have come across: pulse grazing, rational grazing, holistic grazing. Whatever. Carbon sequestration was enough of a vocabulary lesson for one chapter. The idea, though, is that animals are rotated from one area to another, ensuring that grasses and other vegetation being consumed are at an optimal point of growth for both the animal and the land. Once again, this is mimicking relationships found in the natural world. In this very manner, American bison co-evolved with the prairie, and zebras and wildebeests co-evolved with the savannah. Before the grazers have a chance to do damage, they move on and both the animal and land are better off for it. It's quite a beautiful relationship actually. Maybe not as romantic as when talking about domesticated cattle and pigs on a farm, but pretty cool nonetheless.

It's pretty cool that some evidence suggests that ranches exist in which cattle, by grazing sustainably in the above mentioned way, have brought back abundance to land that had previously been exhausted. It's pretty cool that soil that had been compacted, over-exploited, and trampled to the point of being devoid of life can transform into biologically rich meadows by introducing some free-ranging animals. It's pretty cool how grazing livestock can promote an increase in nitrogen fixing plants, photosynthesis, fertilizer, and root biomass. Sepp Holzer is pretty cool. And so it is that healthy pastures, not only rich with biodiversity, can absorb carbon from the atmosphere. There it is. Safe and inexpensive carbon sequestration.

You've heard it before, nature is a web of interdependent strands. The by-product of one process feeds another. Raising animals in a manner that mimics their natural behaviors and interactions with their environment has multiple benefits. Happy, healthy animals are one of those benefits – and not an insignificant one. Happy, healthy humans who care for and eat those happy, healthy animals are another. But not only do Sepp Holzer's pigs provide pork and bacon for his community, there are by-products of this process that not only have zero negative effects on the environment, but actually enrich it. By harnessing biomass, improving the soil and all of its components, cultivating plant life, and offsetting fossil fuel emissions, we are operating in accordance with natural laws.

I'm under no illusion that sustainable livestock grazing is going to stop global climate change. Only billions of people simultaneously stopping the use of fossil fuels will do that. But since *that* isn't going to happen any time soon, we can only find pieces of the puzzle on how to live harmoniously with the land. Politicians, actors, and activists are all talking and talking about healing the planet. There are a couple of very effective ways to do such a thing that, coincidentally or not, involve meat. Hunting. Sustainable livestock. Bioregionalism. The politics of place.

Speaking of which, don't even get me started on the inspiring efforts that non-agricultural hunter-gatherer-horticultural tribes have been engaging in to resist the forces of environmental degradation and to safeguard their homelands. From 500 years of indigenous rebellion against the genocidal colonization of the Americas, to the other side of the world where the Jharnia – the "protectors of the streams" – waged direct action against a global mining company that was attempting to destroy the sacred mountains, forests, and rivers on which they depend. There are inspiring stories of native resistance to environmental imperialism across the globe. I keep saying we have a thing or two to learn from these folks.

Bioregionalism is self, community, *and* environmental defense, all at the same time.

***

The sun was shining. The birds were chirping. Reggae music was in the air and people were having picnics under pavilions while some sat by the pond enjoying the serenity of the evening. We had come to the park so the boys could ride their new scooters that their grandmother had just bought them. We had walked down to the pond ourselves to see if we could spot any fish in the shallow water when we noticed the injured mallard.

At a distance, we thought maybe it was deformed or had a broken leg. Upon closer examination, it was tangled up in fishing line, with the hook through its tongue.

We were able to catch the duck, and untangle its legs and wing from the line. My wife held it down, while I tried to remove the hook as gently as possible. This was no small hook, which made me wonder who and why someone would be fishing using this hook in a pond inhabited by mostly bluegills, sunfish, and small bass. But either way, it had a barb that could secure a damn Atlantic Salmon. Even a duck apparently. The mandible beak had already been torn to shreds with holes. That hook wasn't coming out easily.

We decided I would go home, get a couple tools, and she would stay securing the duck. And that's when the storm clouds came in. By the time I had returned, it was pouring. My family was huddled in a small gazebo drenched, and my wife was squatting holding a duck, covered in blood and duck diarrhea.

On a different day, in a different setting, I may just have shot this duck and roasted it with onions and sweet potatoes without a second thought. But this day, we felt a moral obligation of sorts to save this duck, a victim of human irresponsibility. The wind was picking up though. Lightening and thunder crashing all around. Hail, the size of quarters started whipping down. Kids crying, all of us shivering from the cold of the high winds and heavy downpours. The poor duck, bleeding and pooping. This was not just any storm. We're talking flash floods. Cars stalled in the streets. Puddles up to my knees. We're talking *violence*. And we were stuck outside in it. And I still could not get the damn hook out of this duck's tongue.

So I sliced the neck of that duck right off as quickly as I could. While my wife held down its wings, I took my knife and instantly decapitated it. We brought it home, processed it, and cooked it up a couple days later. I feel it was the most humane thing to do, to end the suffering of this helpless bird and honor it by feeding its nutrients to my family. I've tried to imagine what I would have done if I had still been vegan. It was a weekend evening, in the middle of the most intense storm of the summer, with no wildlife rehabilitator or veterinarian around to help. When I was vegan, I wouldn't have been comfortable enough with wildlife to even get close enough to handle it and try to remove the hook. I certainly wouldn't have been able to end its life. I wouldn't have known how even if I could have. There is no doubt in my mind that it would have sat there in its own feces, being pelted with rain and hail, bleeding to death slowly.

Animal rights activists do not have a monopoly on having empathy for our non-human relations. In fact, historically, it has been hunters who have fulfilled this role. The moral of this experience is perhaps not an obvious one. It speaks to my belief that we are meant to be participants in this world, not spectators. It does us good to once in a while be exposed to the elements, as well as our misgivings; they both help teach us to once again trust in the order of life. And I believe it is the case, be it with the flu or industrial agriculture, once one begins to empower themselves by taking a degree of responsibility, opening up to something larger, and acting accordingly, suffering can slowly be replaced with recovery.

***

Modern humans are by and large insulated from the processes of their ecosystems, especially isolated from death. We do everything in our power to deny death despite the fact that we have never been and can never be above this process. This aversion to life and death is a product of a dominionist agricultural-based culture where natural habitat was seen as an enemy to farms.

It may have started with fairytales of deep, dark forests inhabited with wolves, bears and bogeymen.

But its not so innocent anymore when our children now suffer from obesity, attention deficit disorders, and depression at unprecedented levels because they don't go outside and play. We must realize that poor physical health, in addition to despondency and loss of vitality, is unique to civilized man and domesticated animals.

In non-civilized societies, nutritional deficiency is an occasional result of seasonal change or other short-term ecological disruptions. Mental illness and environmental destruction are rare. In fact, I recently read about how attempts to study depression in non-agricultural societies have simply found nothing to study. In our society, these maladies are chronic and extensive to say the least. No other animal acts and feels like this until put into a cage or a zoo or when their land and culture is ripped away from them by invaders and abusers. Widespread illness is just one portion of the price we will pay for our allegiance to those invaders and abusers. Thus, the corporate executive with his suit and technological gadgets and microwavable lunch, in fact, *is* living in perfect balance with his environment; it cannot be any other way. As is the suburban mom, with her new spacious cookie cutter tract house, who hates what her life has been reduced to. Obesity. Anxiety disorders. Maybe everything is in perfect harmony after all ... which is precisely *why* we suffer.

But I don't want to suffer. And although we've been fooled into thinking otherwise, there is no reason to think we need to stay faithful to the entity that is destroying us and our only home. Yes, a sickness exists that has infected our entire society. But there are antidotes right within our grasp. One, we need to reduce our addiction to industrial civilization. The other, once again if you didn't catch it, we need to simply interact with the natural world and its processes. Honestly, these two prescriptions are one in the same and can take many forms. We'll get back to meat in a minute, but for a moment, I want to discuss biophilia.

Biophilia is the love of life, the instinctual bond between humans and the rest of the community of life. It has been studied and documented and our vitality depends upon it. Most of us have an innate affinity for nature, which is exemplified by the the way we adore baby animals, find indescribable beauty in waterfalls or mountains, or hang pictures of flowers and landscapes on our walls. In fact, biophilia is evident in too many ways to list. But most who recognize the existence and importance of biophilia fail to take it a step further. There can be no embracing life without simultaneously and necessarily embracing death. There can be no love without participation and engagement.

There are many hobbies and pursuits that take modern individuals and put them in a more "natural" habitat, of course, usually in the summer when the weather is more predictably agreeable. While there may be benefits, some of which I mentioned above, many of these activities are still largely passive. Hiking and bird-watching are nice, but honestly are more the equivalent of walking through a museum with objects on display, not to be touched or otherwise interacted with. Mountain biking or backpacking are more active, but how much are we noticing or relating to as we scramble from point A to point B? Hunting, wilderness skills, gardening, and raising livestock not only take people into the outdoors, but also involve participation with the other components of an ecosystem. They require attentiveness, awareness, and interaction. The hunter or horticulturist is not merely on the land, he or she is a fundamental and integral part of it, partaking in its cycles.

And so here we return, once again, to meat.

One who takes possession of the process of providing meat for their family receives the health benefits of fresh air, sunshine (or rain, or snow) on their skin, which cultivates awareness and stimulates the body and all of its sensations. I contend that reaching in and feeling the warmth of blood and organs with our bare hands as we gut the creature that will nourish our family is good for the human soul. After all, the most sensual experience that many people have in this day and age is typing on a computer with our bare hands for hours on end at work, just so we can go home and type on a computer all night to relax.

By engaging in a process such as hunting, he or she is contributing to the enrichment of their environment in multiple ways. Bioregional meat, without even trying to be, becomes an act of self-defense and environmental protection. And in the end, as if the process was not valuable enough with all these boons to our health and our world, the end product is one of a nutritional quality for our physical body unparalleled by other conventional food items.

And so considering the undertaking that lies before us when it comes to healing ourselves and our sick and fragmented relationship to the natural world, I have to ask a series of questions. The questions are directed to those who would, despite hundreds of thousands of years of kinship between humans, their prey, and the land, *still* claim: "meat is murder." What is more akin to murder? Mindfully transforming flesh from one creature into another, or gradually and sometimes very painfully committing suicide in a toxic, detached, artificial technology controlled existence?

Is it the gardeners, homesteaders, hunters, or people otherwise killing and butchering their own meat, who are living backwards? Are they primitive? Barbarians? Savage? How many of us know the kind of attunement required to stalk a prey animal or the degree of consideration and compassion required to take the life of an animal our children helped to raise? The more relevant question is can the sensual experiences that come with intimately interacting with living beings in this way be *healing*? I think the evidence suggests that it does. I think it is very possible that acquiring and eating meat is a manifestation of biophilia.

The million-dollar question of our generation is this: where do sanity and wellness reside and how can we attain some semblance of them?

It may be reassuring to realize that though we may feel and act disconnected or alienated from the natural world, in reality, we can never be so. We are not above ecological reality. We are sensual and curious animals (not mechanized devices) and have evolved to be so. With such loneliness, stress, physical degeneration and environmental destruction, we need to remember *where we come from* in order to heal our relationship to the land.

Meat as medicine. Who knew?

8. SURVIVAL

"Adapt to the harshness, or become one with the dust."

Earth Crisis

I suppose it is at the beginning of the last chapter that I am to start articulating a message of hope so you can put this book down and feel motivated and inspired. I do have an agenda, after all. I'll even spell it out for you so there is no misconstruing the message of the last seven chapters.

I want to defend hunting as a spiritual and healing subsistence strategy. Along those lines, I want to recruit more compassionate hunters, especially young men who have few healthy outlets for their own genetic inclinations. I want to appeal to the foodies and locavores, who already recognize the bankruptcy of the industrial food system, to take their conviction to the next level towards a community-based food economy. I want to illustrate alternatives other than abstinence from meat, which may not be the healthiest option, so that conscientious folks who rightly abhor animal abuse can make sound choices for their bodies and their families. And though this book is about food, I can't help but use this opportunity to articulate our obligation to the immediate end of our civilization's war on earth-based cultures.

Is that too tall an order?

So, considering all these motives, I suppose in the end, I should not leave my readers feeling cynical and helpless. I'll give that a shot. But first I have to admit that I've learned some things over the years about population dynamics, carrying capacity, mortality rates, and such. The only logical conclusion to come to is that the collapse of our civilization is inevitable. We have progressed to a point, whether intentionally or not, where we have completely taken for granted our own life support systems. When connection to the land and its creatures is no longer appreciated, when the primordial vibration that flows through all things can no longer be felt, when dreams are ignored, that is when deterioration begins. This process of disintegration has been in motion for thousands of years and cannot continue indefinitely. And the clincher is that most people still don't have a clue that this has even happened, let alone know what to do about it.

Pick up any wildlife biology text you can find and I'd bet it will tell you, in no uncertain terms, that any given habitat can only support a limited population of a given species. An increase above this limit cannot be sustained and will lead to eventual crash. The fact that we humans wear ties and drive SUV's and have smartphones does not exempt us from this self-regulating system. It actually only expedites the process. It could come from our own hands intentionally dismantling our own culture, or, as an unchosen consequence of our collective transgressions. But either way, our current way of life *will* come to an end.

I recognize that science is little more than widely accepted mythology and, while perhaps quite useful at times, is not always the authority. We don't need methodical empirical study to predict collapse. The impending end of our empire can be felt on a deep emotional level to those who choose to be attuned to their environments, as we fall further into despair and disease. Either way, even everything our sciences have discovered about biological and ecological law points to a potentially grim reality. The evidence is overwhelming. This cannot be ignored in favor of just leaving you with a feel-good message.

Like the Gaia hypothesis mentioned earlier that recognizes this planet acting as if it is a living organism, our culture acts as if it is a living sociopath. One that cannot be reasoned with or redeemed. Here it is. I'll say it. I don't have much hope. Like prayer, hope is overrated, and sometimes dangerous.

But once we get over waiting and hoping for something different to magically happen, we can see that there is a positive message that can nonetheless be gleaned from the facts, even knowing how dire they truly are. At *any point*, we have the choice to walk away, as did the cultures long before us who traded in agricultural life for something more meaningful. We can have the courage and clarity to face reality, while choosing *not* to live in despair and disease. *The end of civilization does not mean lack of a future.* Quite the contrary.

You can't negotiate with a sociopath, but you sure as hell can starve one to death.

If nothing else, there are steps we can take to soften the blow of collapse; to buy more time for our children and grandchildren to make the choices we did not have the courage to make. Sometimes, as much as my two children are the most important thing in the world to me, I feel a pang of regret bringing them into this world and the one they are inheriting. I can only aspire to do my part so that the coming cultural transition can happen more smoothly, rather than catastrophically for them and their offspring. This is possible if people can begin to open their eyes to the crimes being committed by the institutions that drive civilization, and admit accountability for their own passivity.

I am not an authority on these matters. I am far away from living in a sustainable way myself. There are so many areas – physically, spiritually, and mentally – left to re-wild within me. However, I am optimistic that hunting, gathering, and mindfully managing the growth of some of the food that ends up on the dinner plate are tools that I can pass on to my children, to gain a bit of self-sufficiency, self-worth, and compassion towards the whole of life. Regaining land-based skills and increasing our nature literacy is something that can *only* lead to liberation in one form or another. In turn, we can then all contribute to a community willing to build anew.

After all, when the shit hits the fan, do you want to be a fit, cunning, and skillful huntsman and trapper? A wise horticulturist skilled in the art of holistic and humane animal husbandry? Or a malnourished vegetarian looting health food stores for half rotten-tofu?

The origins of our failure as a civilization cannot be separated from the way in which we produce food. In fact, agriculture as we know it is *the* defining characteristic of our culture. But as we have seen, our style of food production has been the impetus for our current environmental crisis, as well as our health crisis … as well as our spiritual crisis … as well as our political crisis … as well as our economic crisis….

If you've read this far, you have gotten the point by now.

Could it logically follow that if food production was the impetus for this mess, the way we acquire our food could be a possible path *away* from this mess? In ecology, succession is the process by which one community of living things is replaced by another. Cultural succession could then be described as the replacement of one *culture* by another. So what drives the process of cultural succession? After years of considering these types of questions, it seems to me that what could drive that process is a shift in subsistence strategies.

Considering our ancestral roots, which is always a good idea when it comes to our well-being and that of the planet, we should be asking the question of whether and to what degree hunting and tending livestock could have a role in this movement. In order to answer that question, we could look at some of the recent successes in the efforts to connect people with sustainably grown produce.

The fact is that we are living in a period of time where, whether because of either fad or growth of consciousness, increasing numbers of people are beginning to withdraw support for an unsustainable food system. Albeit little by little, people may just be waking up to the notion that these problems may have a root cause. With a little agitation of the system, that awakening can be expanded upon in a sort of positive feedback loop. Maybe.

***

Not long ago, I was sitting uncomfortably in a chair at the dentist's office while his assistant was cleaning my teeth – or should I say attacking me. While poking and scraping around in my mouth, she began inquiring about community supported agriculture options in our area. She knew that we kept backyard hens and were founding members of an urban chicken keeping club and thus she figured I would probably be hip to the CSA's around and could give advice on which to join. If you have been living either in a closet or Mississippi and haven't heard, CSA's are based upon a model where a household purchases a share of a farmer's crops for the season. In turn they receive local, in-season produce each week from that farm for the duration of the growing season. It is an arrangement that financially supports local farmers as well as involves consumers with the source of their food. It's a wonderful model in many ways. And my dentist wanted in on the fun.

A woman who is a grandmother, white and suburban as can be and conventional in every American way, wanting in on food activism. Really?

Really. These once radical ideas are not so radical anymore. Healthier food is becoming mainstream due to the collective efforts of small-scale farmers, food activists and consumers. One no longer has to have dreadlocks, or be an anti-consumerist, or smell like patchouli to be out there espousing the benefits of organic vegetables and CSA's.

This growing movement towards local and less environmentally damaging foods can be seen in the trend towards organic and small-scale family farms. According to the United States Department of Agriculture, there were 7,175 farmers markets registered in the United States in 2011. Over 1000 of those opened since 2010. Over 5000 have opened since the mid-1990's. The demand for chemical free food, in particular, is sharply on the rise in recent years. This is reflected in the fact that organic food is the fastest growing sector of the food industry. These sorts of statistics point to the fact that more and more people are beginning to care where their food comes from every year.

But many of us know that a trend such as this is not enough. And while food issues are currently captivating the mainstream, we need to go beyond organic. Considering the damage we have wrought, we need to even go beyond sustainable. While organic agriculture is a step in the right direction, in and of itself, it does not suffice to address all of the ramifications of industrial agriculture. It is true that these types of trends may soften the destructive force that is industrial agriculture and provide a foundation that could support even better ideas. However, the organic food movement is finding itself at a crossroads between its original alternative principles of holistic and healthy farming, and being usurped by industrial agriculture.

Unlike "organic," which is a subjective standard, bioregional perspectives about food – based on simplicity, place, and *true* sustainability – do not lend themselves to large-scale implementation. So, for the foreseeable future, they will continue to exist outside the margins. Eventually, more people will realize how empowering producing their own food is. As local communities begin to reclaim food sovereignty, those threatened super-sized institutions will either try to stop the momentum through government regulation or commercialize any gains that have been made by selling it back to us. But they will not succeed this time.

No matter how crafty marketers may be, they cannot make small-scale large-scale. There are only so many deer in the woods. You can only fit so many grass-fed cattle in a pasture. Only so much money can be made promoting foraging, urban gardens, and raising backyard goats. The Piggery doesn't lend itself to being a chain restaurant. And on top of that, there are countless bioregions that will develop their own unique food systems. For the first time in decades, at least from within the confines of our own civilization, human communities will be calling the shots – not multinational corporations. And then, as I have suggested, things might just get interesting.

For now, I think we should remain critical of convention and suspicious of large-scale entities, even when it comes to less destructive food production. I think, without necessarily drawing a definite conclusion, that it's worth exploring whether it's a good thing or not that Walmart even has a natural foods section. Even most natural food stores are filled with products and supplements, not real food. Is it a "good" thing when the global food industry conspires with the global environmental movement to clear endless tracts of rainforest for organic farming, in order to feed snobby westerners? Despite my criticism, I will be the first to acknowledge that some answers have begun to emerge with the growing interest in organically produced food. But I still also acknowledge that those answers tend to come from the more radical contingent of the socially just and environmentally friendly food movements.

It is the fringes of society where transitions begin. In ecology, it is the edges of a given habitat that are most productive and contain the most diversity. And where these answers sprout from, whether by name or not, is almost always a bioregional approach to growing food. Some of us realize that organic does not necessarily fall under this umbrella, and neither does most of the other food found in the "natural" food section of your local grocery or department store. After all, bioregionalism is a philosophy that views humans as participants, rather than masters, in their local biotic community. It emphasizes local economies and in doing so, ensures that as participants, we need to maintain and adapt to the local environment, not just avoid chemicals, corn syrup and hydrogenated oil.

Rebecca Spector makes the very essential point in *Fatal Harvest*: "Bioregionalism suggests that people tend to not pollute or damage the natural system on which they depend for their livelihood if they participate in and see directly what is happening to that natural system." Derrick Jensen makes the exact same point in the film *What a Way to Go: Life at the End of Empire*: "If your experience is that your food comes from a grocery store and that your water comes from a tap, you will defend to the death the system that brings them to you because your life depends on it. If, on the other hand, your water comes from a stream and your food comes from a land base, you will defend to the death that stream and land base because your life depends upon it."

What these two quotes have in common is that they show a clear understanding of what moves people to care about their environment. And that is key. They are not advocating government or third party certified food. They are in agreement that there is no dichotomy between who we are and where our food comes from. They do not agree with the reliance on outside forces to heal our relationships to the ecological systems we are undeniably a part of. We, and the food that we are made of, are strands of the same web. And when we see ourselves as such, we will conserve, nurture, and protect our interests.

A bioregional approach to food production thus would ensure that greater consideration be granted to every aspect of the ecology of a region. The natural community *itself* would present the most suitable model for agricultural practices. Bioregionalism is simply a new name for a practice that indigenous cultures have engaged in for eons. And this is the approach, in one form or another, that they have applied when manipulating the environment for preferred foods.

Contrarily, most modern farmers are engaged in a veritable battle with the natural world that they cannot win. There are ecological processes taking place on every parcel of land across the planet, and as the evidence continually proves, working against these processes is an uphill battle. Agriculturists unsuccessfully attempt to defeat nature with technology. They must constantly apply biocides to eliminate unwanted plants, animals, and fungi that continue to grow naturally. Synthetic nutrients must be added to the soil to bypass the nutrient cycles that have been interrupted. Annual plants are forced to grow where perennial forests or prairie should, so these human-created environments are very fragile. Natural ecosystems are healthy and resilient.

In summary, bioregionalism provides a new model for food subsistence that goes beyond growing crops without synthetic chemicals or raising livestock on organic feed. One that is not susceptible to be co-opted by agribusiness. What is needed is a model of food production, both plant and animal, that mimics the time-tested processes of a given local ecosystem.

***

We need not look far and wide. One of the most promising movements in recent years is the permaculture movement, which incorporates ecological principles to grow food and design human settlements. Essentially, it is a form of biomimicry, which is why it has such potential as a philosophy. Biomimicry is simply the emulation of natural patterns and strategies to solve a particular problem, such as how the invention of Velcro was inspired by the seed heads of burdock. Therefore, its application to acquiring food would involve asking how food naturally grows in a particular place. Permaculture relies on polycultures, perennials, agroforestry and a host of other ecological and biological principles. It is a bioregional approach, as it seeks to integrate the land with its inhabitants. A permaculture system recycles wastes, reduces labor and incorporates animals and plants together, as in a healthy ecosystem. A permaculture system *is* a healthy ecosystem, diverse and stable. It is the modern day antithesis of industrial agriculture. It is a place-based, rather than profit-based system.

As far as it relates to humans cultivating food – as opposed to hunting and foraging for it – the aim of permaculture can essentially be described as "farming in nature's image." But from my vantage point, most of the many wonderful and inspirational grassroots efforts to change the state of food production in this country still revolve around *plant* foods. From seed savers, urban community gardens, underground bread cooperatives to dumpster divers, mushroom foragers, and farmers' markets – the examples are plentiful. To be fair, there is a growing awareness and market for grass-fed beef and other pastured livestock. But for all the achievements of the various food movements, demand and supply for affordable, authentic, sustainably and humanely raised meat is not growing at a proportional rate to that of veggies.

I own a couple of full-length books about permaculture, each of which have only a couple pages dealing with animals. If we are to recognize the many philosophical and nutritional shortcomings of a strict vegetarian diet, if we are to embrace our paleolithic physicality, then that is not enough. Can we apply these same permaculture principles to acquiring meat? More efforts could be put forth to unlock the knowledge of acquiring and processing animal food. Can we begin to *hunt* in nature's image as well? This is exactly where sustenance hunting fits in. And when hunting is not the ecological option, can meat animals be raised with the same considerations as a polyculture guild of complementary plants that serve multiple functions? This is where permaculture and other similar systems fit in.

Another related and promising remedy to many of our ailments lies in what has come to be called regenerative design. It not only offers an answer to the question of how we could feed ourselves sustainably, but a host of other questions that we should be asking. Regenerative design, like permaculture, is ancestral wisdom given a modern name by people who have rediscovered its importance in the face of the world we live in. If there is a lifeline for our children as our culture drowns, I'm pretty confident that regenerative design is an integral part of it.

I have made the case elsewhere in this book that one of the defining characteristics of our species is that we are designers. Honey bees are engineers. Beavers build dams. Peregrine falcons hunt on the wing. And human beings design. Whether it is the invention of tools to make friction fire 100,000 years ago, or the engineering of solid oxide fuel cell devices for our vehicles in modern times, it's what we do. As a whole, we are an ingenious type of animal. Unfortunately, our inventiveness – having been severed from a land ethic – has gotten us into a lot of trouble. But there is no reason that it cannot once again be used in a healthy way.

The basis of regenerative design then is that not only can humans live, design, and create in a way that is not destructive to the environment, but any of our actions can serve to enhance the land that is enhancing our well being. In this way, humans are not a scourge upon the landscape, but a healing agent. When creating tools, settlements, social systems, and meeting other human needs, we can actually revitalize the resources we are using. Regenerative design has been applied in innovative ways to buildings, food systems, craftsmanship, homeschooling programs and philosophies, ceremony and so much more.

The time is long overdue that we reawaken to the fact that we, as a species, have a place in the order of life. If we didn't, we wouldn't be here. Once we come to that recognition, we can respond accordingly. This is what the proponents of modern movements such as permaculture and regenerative design are attempting to do. We can tune in to the connections that were as central to our ancestors' existence as walking and breathing. We can relearn the skills and design processes necessary to create local food economies.

***

As much as I'd like to keep patting regenerative design on the back, the zillion dollar question here is how do these philosophies, as beautiful and meaningful as they are on paper, specifically apply to putting meatloaf, roasted chicken, or even woodchuck burgers on the table?

The easy answer is that it depends upon your bioregion. The other easy answer is that it depends upon peoples' ability and willingness to get creative. Both of these answers are true, but if you've gotten this far in this book, you're probably not going to let me off the hook that easily. Luckily, though creativity has never been a particular strength of mine, I can at least recognize it when I see it and can hint at a few examples other than Sepp Holzer.

I've seen small-scale vegetable farms nearly destroyed due to the appetites of hungry critters. In my bioregion and ones with similar attributes, the culprits are deer, woodchucks, rabbits – wildlife species that thrive off certain forms of human settlements and the farms that make them possible. I used to live in a neighborhood that was literally infested with gray squirrels. There was no chance for successful gardening there. It's just too painful seeing every fruit on a tree disappear in one night or a strawberry patch that was raided. And I wasn't even trying to make a living off my gardens as much as get some homegrown treats once in a while.

I know one organic farmer who claimed to me that he killed sixty deer on his own land in one growing season. And he obviously didn't eat anywhere close to the majority of them, nor did he donate the meat to a local food bank. I've heard of other similar stories of farmers driving around in ATVs or tractors with a shotgun at their side, picking off deer whenever they cross paths, letting the deer rot where they dropped dead. Small farmers cannot compete with large agribusiness operations who are so big, they either have elaborate electric fences or so many acres and acres of crops, that a handful of pesky mammals can't make a dent.

However, as discouraging and maddening as it is, in all these cases these furry fruit and veggie eating critters were doing exactly what they are designed and driven to do – eat as the opportunity presents itself. Which is *precisely* what *we* should be doing by eating *them*. Rather than farmers taking justice into their own hands and potentially acting in irresponsible ways in defense of their livelihood, what about encouraging more creative guidelines and regulations for hunting?

I'd love to conduct research on the wide variability of indigenous hunting strategies in temperate climates and see how they could be applied to out-of-balance pest species today. Not only do certain species damage human crops, but they feed on seedlings and sensitive populations of plants, altering the composition of vegetation of an area in adverse ways. Either way, in the absence of predators, it is obvious that many ecological systems today could benefit from more hunting. Hunters could collaborate with their local small-scale farms. Nuisance animal permits could be signed over to non-resident hunters in exchange for a share of the farm. Likewise, many municipalities are struggling with deer overpopulation problems and state employees or police sometimes carry out controversial bait and shoot programs, where meat is usually wasted.

In either case, the solutions could be handed over to food activists and hunters, and processing of the meat could evolve into a community event. Families would help with the butchering as an educational experience and, in return, take home some ground venison. Wilderness skills instructors could teach children how to tan hides and then they could make crafts from the hides and antlers.

Along these lines, I wonder about the formation of wild food collectives in each bioregion. These gatherings could address the human need for and benefits of wild foods, including meat. Participants could work cooperatively to teach about wild edibles, ethical harvesting, and protecting habitat. Members could barter amongst themselves or with other collectives in other bioregions. Wild food potlucks can be organized. I'll trade you guys some rabbit stew for some wild rice. No? Cattail shoots for grouse then. Entomophagy clubs. Fishing parties. Bow making workshops. The possibilities are end-less.

I also believe it is important to note, when considering what a bioregional food economy could look like, that history doesn't support the notion of self-sufficiency. Yes, there is something romantic about the homesteading lifestyle, but in the end, self-sufficiency is overrated. It may be better than the conventional alternative, but I argue food is not supposed to be provided by either a corporation *or* the self. The principles of regenerative design are more efficiently applied with the assistance of community involvement. This is how cultural succession could unfold – by working collectively on projects, respecting the knowledge of our elders, and mentoring our children in the traditional ecological knowledge of our particular place.

I don't know exactly what this would look like for you. Perhaps you are a single mother living in the Midwest, struggling to make ends meet. Maybe you are a young punk rock kid from the Northwest trying to find your place in the world. Perhaps you are living on a commune or in a ghetto. But I think it's safe to suggest that bioregionalism looks not only like changing our relationship to the natural world and the species upon which we depend, but also changing our relationship to each other. Yes, part of the bioregional approach to acquiring meat is community building. Whether it be villagers in South America that work together on a turtle conservation project to ensure a food supply during seasonal floods, or the Malaysian tribe mentioned in an earlier chapter that celebrate as a community over a meal of fire-roasted monkey. Traditional cultures around the world approach meat communally because animals are held in high esteem and, as such, are often honored.

What about cells of permaculture activists that experiment in various forms of mischievous guerilla gardening? What about the establishment of edible forest gardens through land trusts where animals would be integrated? What about ecological design meet-ups for neighborhoods? Pastured meat buying clubs or meat CSA projects? Bartering backyard livestock? Underground supper clubs operating outside the confines of government regulations? I can't help envisioning how far these types of projects could take us away from the industrial model of food production. We could effectively put a halt to factory farming by community building – one chicken or pig at a time. We could cut out transportation costs, reduce and eventually eliminate fossil fuel use, and keep costs down *while* supporting the local economy and ecology.

I had a conversation recently with someone about what the heck a permaculture meat farm would even look like. I prefer to set the stage by reframing it as a permaculture meat garden (or more simply – a *garden*!). And though the term "meat garden" sounds a bit weird and degrading on the surface, what we truly need is more community gardens and fewer farms.

To me, that looks like a balance of habitat types more than anything else. It looks like a juxtaposition of different stages of ecological succession, productively managed by human hands. It looks like agroforestry. In the temperate northeastern states, it may look like pasture working in conjunction with woodlands, with plenty of edge habitat to increase biodiversity. No more forests would be lost to farming, because resources – including animals – would be harvested from woodlands in accordance to sustainable principles. Habitat appropriate species would be raised and fed from perennial feeding systems. In fact, though such a "farm" could be managed for meat, no natural system serves only one purpose. A permaculture meat garden could grow huge amounts of food, medicine, fuel and fiber, regardless of the taxonomic kingdoms categorized by biologists.

The Cayuga Basin bioregion of which I am a part is composed of much old fields and thickets. Goats, as browsers, would thrive in this sort of habitat. Rabbits, ducks, geese, turkey, and pheasants all live in the wild here, so would be suitable to raise in this area with a minimum of human interference. Animals related to these species – guinea fowl, quail, and partridges – could also do well in such a permaculture garden. Pigs, in balanced numbers, thrive in the forest. Heritage varieties of sheep and other hardy grazers could forage on pastures that are not so large as to infringe upon the forest.

The beauty of any ecologically designed project is that it doesn't look the same here as it does elsewhere. This is the principle of bioregionalism and all the diversity, creativity and resilience that it offers those that honor the fact. I simply am scratching the surface of what may be possible in the environment in which I live to serve as an example. The point is to observe the natural world and its patterns, connect with it and use *that* as a model, rather than the factory model that has been the norm for too damn long now.

As trends change, a subtle shift toward approaches such as permaculture, and its sister regenerative design, may be slowly taking place. And if so, we as a culture will realize a few facts concerning food. Humans fed themselves sustainably for hundreds of thousands of years of our evolution.

Isolated populations of native people living off their land base still exist (for now) as models of a sustainable food system. Agriculture is a recent invention. Industrial agriculture is practically a brand new development. There are other strategies for subsistence. Food production does not have to be in conflict with all that is wild, and farms and gardens can exist as natural habitats in flow with the surrounding ecosystem.

Alternatives do exist, but first we have to abandon the one that is wreaking havoc on the environment we absolutely and unequivocally depend upon in every way. When we embrace bioregionalism, agriculture as we know it will cease to exist. It is only then that the degradation caused by agriculture, in all its forms, can begin to heal. It is only then that conditions will be ripe for cultural succession.

***

I've encountered many environmental and food activists who support hunting in theory. I've seen Weston Price followers place "wanted" adds on Craigslist for venison and other wild game, but simultaneously claim they wouldn't pull the trigger. I cannot tell you how many people I've talked to about meat and raising animals who say that they could never take a life. These are usually folks who eat meat too. And considering our reference from within the confines of civilization, I don't necessarily blame them.

But is this rational or healthy? As we know, the food we eat literally becomes us – spiritually speaking and physically on a molecular level. "Matter cycles continuously through the web of life." "You are what you eat." These are biologically true statements. Hippie philosopher Alan Watts said it better than I can when he wrote, "We are other creatures rearranged." Meat eating is as much *giving* life to the predator as it is taking it from the prey. It is a transfer on an energetic and biological level from one being to another. This same process takes place when harvesting plants.

In other words, if you simply eat, you kill. This is irrefutable. Even fruitarians and raw vegans kill – it's just their own bodies that they are slowly murdering. It is certainly an option for us to pass this deed off to anonymous parties who treat plants and, in this case, animals like machines. In fact, almost all of us do to one extent or another. But not only is this giving a green light to unaccountable abuse, we miss out on the rewards that come from partaking in these processes ourselves. Most of us have no meaningful relationship to our food or the land it comes from. I'd like to see that change. I'd like to see more authenticity when it comes to death, more openness. Greater accountability necessitates greater conscientiousness. Can you take a life to feed your family? Thousands of generations of our ancestors did.

I've debated back and forth whether to include this analogy that I've used before, but what the hell – I'm not trying to win any awards here. If you are not into evolutionary biology, you can think of it like this. Defecating in the woods. Your domesticated self surely resists the foreign idea. The civilized part of you cringes at the thought of squatting down with your drawers dropped and having your business dropped anywhere but in a porcelain bowl like proper citizens do it. The flies. The mosquitoes. No toilet paper? But make no mistake, inside, the animal within wants to squat and let nature take over and do what it does so well. In the end, it is liberating. You may not want to go back to that cold hard toilet seat where your body gets so contorted. Because it is liberating to act like the animal you are.

Yes, you are an animal. Can you not only read about where your food comes from or watch a documentary, but also physically witness and partake in that process? Squeamishness aside, most of us are busy and stressed. Likewise, most of us do not have mountains of disposable income or energy. There are justifiable challenges and hurdles to creating a local, ethical, and decentralized food economy. But that challenge is destined to be met, one way or another. It will be hard now or harder – if not devastating – later. So, yes, you can do it.

With a little intention, you can.

I began learning to hunt on my own in my thirties with no experience, no mentor, no gun, and no land. I currently live in a cohousing community allowing me to more easily partake in the types of projects I am interested in. My family moved here – on purpose – to a place with like-minded neighbors, acres of healthy land, in a city notorious for being on the crest of the local and sustainability movements. If things were to ever get ugly, I feel we are in an advantageous position. I'm not particularly lucky and this was no accident. One of the first things I did upon moving here was put forth a proposal to allow members to hunt in designated areas of our 120 cooperatively owned acres. Not long after, we started raising meat chickens. And further plans for permaculture-inspired food projects are on the horizon at the time of writing this chapter. Hot Italian goat sausage coming up….

There is nothing special about me, my family, or my community when it comes to capability. We just made a choice to be here and embark on this journey. Similar choices await every sentient, free-willed human who wants something more than what our culture of occupation offers.

A culture, not only of occupation, but which is also a sadistic thief. It has stolen our humanity, our experiences, our skills and fooled us into thinking we are helpless and dependent. It has committed – and continues to commit – heinous crimes against our animal relations, our ancestors, and most land-based people left. It has left us with empty souls, poor diets, and debilitated bodies. This is unacceptable. This is neither normal nor inevitable.

Hunting, shooting, archery, tracking, tending live-stock … these skills are attainable regardless of where you live or your upbringing. They can be done with family and friends, and you can immerse yourself to any level that is appropriate for you. But it is *you* that must make the first step. Visit a pro shop, search the internet, attend a wilderness skills class, call or visit a shooting range or farm and most importantly, ask questions. Begin talking to people. Put yourself and your intentions out there.

There are a lot of areas in life that allow for each of us to make excuses. And we all do. But times call for a more deliberate way of living. That means less excuses and more action. It simply doesn't serve us to live in denial. It doesn't serve us to talk about enlightenment, peace, and saving the earth if we neglect our very strong and real roots as animal inhabitants of this land. We are animals that kill to live like all others. Our aversion to taking a life for subsistence is not a sign of compassion or progress. By the conventional definition of the word, this very type of "progress" has caused quite a lot of pain to animals both human and non-human alike.

It is possible to take the steps. You can poop in the woods. You can pull the trigger. You can slit the figurative throat of our culture and the literal throat of your prey. And you will be living more fully and compassionately when you do.

***

Do I have time for one more cliché? Indulge me, there are only a few more paragraphs left and then you can put this book down and get a midnight snack of some pemmican or head cheese.

I have come to be a strong proponent of cultivating our oneness with the order of life. And when I say that, I want to be clear that I'm not talking about the whole New Age concept of one love, one people, one whatever. I'm simply talking about recognizing and respecting an existing relationship, not creating a universal culture based on love and goodwill. When I talk about cultivating our oneness with the order of life, I'm talking about a personal and community journey to blend more with our local environment. I'm talking about a growth in awareness and a diminishment of the loud concentric ripples those of our culture tend to create as we pound our way through the landscape gobbling up resources. I'm wondering what could happen.

What could happen when more people take up a shotgun or a compound bow and go and kill their dinner with their own hands? What could happen when more people embrace the empowering and sensual experience that is raising food for themselves, their families, and their communities? What could happen when more people are healthy and strong, rather than sick and passive, from enriching their bodies with real nutrients? What could happen if more people cherished life because they have enriched their souls by satisfying their instincts? Could we live lighter on the land?

Our whole civilization is founded upon this notion that it is our destiny and obligation to control and dominate life for our own needs. Whether its the chicken in the battery farm that is so confined it cannot even move its wings, the steer at the feedlot stuck in piles of its own feces, or a climax forest clearcut for an organic soybean monocrop, intensive agricultural operations are stifling the world in too many ways to count. Ecological principles dictate that this madness cannot continue.

By choice or by force of natural law, our relationship to food production will change. Meat has a definite, if not necessary, place in any healthy strategy to acquire our food in harmony with the natural processes that characterize our bioregions. Given the state of our environmental condition, we cannot buy our way out of this. Something has to happen on a deeper level. Hunting, food cultivation, and other land-based activities offer clarity. Many needs that we have, that may not otherwise be met, are achieved through activities such as these.

Without a basic understanding of how a living entity is transformed into the food we put into our mouths, how can we as a community ever understand the connection between ourselves and the land we inhabit? Humans eat meat and always have. We evolved over millions of years with blood on our hands and reverence in our hearts. This is not about conquering and destroying life. Quite the contrary, it is about healing ourselves and our broken relationship with the land. To acknowledge the fact that in the end, we are all nothing but food is being productive. By doing so, we can emphasize habitat in our lives. We can erase arbitrary borders and tear down the imagined fences of all sorts that confine us. We can eat real food, and slowly starve the factory farm model of meat production. To strive for these things is to embrace authenticity, the animal within, and the role we are adapted for within the greater cycle of life and death.

EPILOGUE

The deer hung from the roof of the shed by her neck, as if to suggest she ended it all because life was just too damn hard. But this premature death wasn't self-induced. It wasn't a result of a bullet or broadhead to her vitals either. No. This beautiful creature's life was unfortunately ended after a violent run in with a 2005 Hyundai Elantra. That would be *my* Hyundai Elantra. It was not the first deer I had accidentally hit with a car. It wasn't the first deer I was going to eat. It was, however, the first deer that I had accidentally hit with a car *and* was going to eat. I believe, if you recall, that I had pointed out elsewhere in this book that simply being out in the woods with a weapon doesn't entitle one to a venison dinner. Boy, isn't that the truth. But sometimes, even during a relative failure of a hunting season, the gods provide venison dinners in unexpected ways.

The unfortunate thing was, the deer didn't die upon impact. The car broke her leg and some ribs which punctured her lung. She sat on the side of the road suffering. I tried to approach with a knife, which was all I had on me, but that didn't go over well. Don't ever try to approach a scared and injured deer. That was the last time I'll try that one. The sheriff came and shot her, putting her out of her misery. Stupid, evil car culture.

Either way, the least that I could do was to put the deer in the stupid, evil car. (I was going to say that putting a deer in your sedan is harder than it sounds, until I realized – it doesn't sound easy either.) If I could bring it home and salvage what meat I could, it would be a much more honorable death than leaving it on the side of the road to suffer, only to die hours later and ultimately be picked up by the transportation department to be thrown in a landfill.

I live in a developing homesteading community. The type of individuals this land attracts tend to be interested in broadening their skill base when it comes to living in a connected way to the land. What I am getting at is that unlike most places, this is one neighborhood that doesn't mind a bloody carcass hanging from the community shed.

As I proceeded to butcher that deer on a frigid November morning, people came by to observe, learn, and partake. One neighbor came by to watch the deer being skinned as he had never seen that process. Another neighbor wanted the liver. Another came by to help my wife cut it up, and was subsequently rewarded with steaks. Someone brought over a food processor so we could make burger. A friend of one boy from our community took the hide to brain tan it. Another took the tail as a souvenir. My own boys took a couple bones to boil and play with as makeshift weapons. Ecofeminists they are not.

My boys.

I will never forget my family's excitement and intrigue when I brought home my first deer on the last weekend of hunting season a few years back. They watched in fascination, taking in all the bloody details of the process of converting mammal into meat for the freezer. While most kids in our culture would cry and turn away in horror seeing their father stained in blood, skinned carcass hanging in the garage – the sights, the smells – these two little boys soaked it all in. My kids know little fear when it comes to this stuff. They know this is where meat comes from. They understand that food comes from the land.

We often look at children as masters of being centered, living in the present with wide eyes. Young children, until about the time they step in public school for the first time, aren't jaded. They aren't typically consumed by fear, but rather by magic. They are uncorrupted. Discovery personified. In short, they are in touch with their instincts. I learn from them all the time, and I consider it our obligation to nurture and mentor them.

That is the main reason I do any of this. It sure as hell is not to save civilization. It's to protect *them*. It's to pass on knowledge that will never otherwise be transmitted by this culture. What they do with any of this knowledge when they are adults is up to them. But I have confidence that, in the very least, they will be familiar with alternatives to this culture of disengagement. The processes of life that govern all of this won't be completely alien. Nature awareness will not be a foreign language like it was to me. I can only hope that I have instilled something, planted a seed, something beautiful. Something sacred. My wish is to contribute to any sort of ripple, no matter how small, that will add to the tidal wave that will eventually wipe away that which is a tumor upon this land.

I never thought I would gain such a feeling of satisfaction seeing the smiles and bright eyes as we turn road-kill into something meaningful – as a community. Perhaps this is because it's a sort of foreshadowing of what is possible to create out of the corpse of our dying culture.

Better than being thrown into a landfill indeed.

This is nourishment.

BIBLIOGRAPHY

Abram, D. (1996). *The spell of the sensuous.* New York, NY: Pantheon Books.

Baur, G. (2008). *Farm sanctuary: changing hearts and minds about animals and food.* New York, NY: Touchstone.

Buell, P., & Girard, J. (2003). *Chemistry fundamentals: an environmental perspective. 2nd ed..* Sudbury, MA: Jones and Bartlett Publishers.

Cartmill, M. (1993). *A view to a death in the morning.* Cambridge, MA: Harvard University Press.

Diamond, J. (1997). *Guns, germs, and steel: the fates of human societies.* New York, NY: W.W. Norton and Company.

Diamond, J. (2005). *Collapse: how societies choose to fail or succeed.* New York, NY: Viking Penguin.

Dizard, J. E. (1994). *Going wild: hunting, animal rights, and the contested meaning of nature.* Amherst, MA: University of Massachusetts Press.

Dowie, M. (2005). *Conservation refugees: the hundred conflict between global conservation and native peoples.* Cambridge, MA: MIT Press.

Eaton, R. L. (1998). *The sacred hunt: hunting as a sacred path.* Ashland, OR: Sacred Press.

Eaton, R. L. (2009). *From boys to men of heart: hunting as rite of passage.* Shelton, WA: OwLink Media.

Fairlie, S. (2010). *Meat: a benign extravagance.* White River Junction, VT: Chelsea Green Publishing.

Feder, K. L., & Park, M. A. 2007. *Human antiquity: an introduction to physical anthropology and archeology. 5th ed.* New York, NY: McGraw-Hill.

Fox, M. W. (1986). *Agricide: the hidden crisis that affects us all.* New York, NY: Schocken Books.

Glendinning, C. (1994). *My name is chellis and I'm in recovery from western civilization*. Boston, MA: Shambala.

Haviland, W. A., Harald P., Walrath D., & McBride B. (2005). *Cultural anthropology: the human challenge. 11th ed.* Toronto: Wadsworth Thomson Learning Inc.

Hartman, T. (2004). *The last hours of ancient sunlight*. New York, NY: Three Rivers Press.

Holzer, S. (2004). *Sepp Holzer's permaculture: a practical guide to small-scale, integrative farming and gardening*. White River Junction, VT: Chelsea Green Publishing.

Jackson, D. L., & Jackson L. L. (2002). *The farm as natural habitat: reconnecting food systems with ecosystems*. Washington, DC: Island Press.

Jensen, D. (2006). *Endgame volume 1: the problem of civilization*. New York, NY: Seven Stories Press.

Katz, S. (2006). *The revolution will not be microwaved: inside America's underground food movements*. VT: Chelsea Green Publishing.

Kimber, R. (2002). *Living wild and domestic: the education of a hunter-gardener*. Guilford, CT: The Lyons Press.

Kimbrell, A. (2002). *Fatal harvest: the tragedy of industrial agriculture*. Washington, DC: Island Press.

Kirby, D. (2010). *Animal factory*. New York, NY: St. Martin's Press.

Kottak, C. P. (2008). *Mirror for humanity: A concise introduction to cultural anthropology. 6th ed.* New York, NY: McGraw-Hill.

Manning, R. (2004). *Against the grain: how agriculture has hijacked civilization*. New York, NY: North Point Press.

Mason, J. (1993). *An unnatural order: uncovering the roots of our domination of nature and each other*. New York, NY: Simon & Schuster.

McNeill, J. R., & McNeill, W. H. (2003). *The human web: a bird's-eye view of world history*. New York, NY: W.W. Norton and Company.

Moran, E. F. (2006). *People and nature: an introduction to human ecological relations.* Malden, MA: Blackwell Publishing.

Nelson, K. (2008). *Original instructions: indigenous teachings for a sustainable future.* Rochester, VT: Bear & Company.

Peterson, D. (1996). *A hunter's heart: honest essays on blood sport.* New York, NY: Henry Holt and Company.

Pyle, G. (2005). *Raising less corn, more hell: the case for the independent farm and against industrial food.* New York, NY: Public Affairs.

Quinn, D. (1999). *Beyond civilization: humanity's next great adventure.* New York, NY: Harmony Books.

Robbins, J. (2001). *The food revolution: how your diet can help save your life and our world.* Berkeley, CA: Conari Press.

Safran-Foer, J. (2009). *Eating animals.* New York, NY: Little Brown and Company.

Sale, K. (1991). *Dwellers in the land: the bioregional vision.* Philadelphia, PA: New Society Publishers.

Singer, P. (1990). *Animal liberation.* New York, NY: The New York Review of Books.

Soule, J. D., & Piper, J. K. (1992). *Farming in nature's image: an ecological approach to agriculture.* Washington: Island Press.

Smith, B. D. (1995). *The emergence of agriculture.* New York, NY: Scientific American Library.

Starr, C. G. (1991). *A history of the ancient world: 4th edition.* New York, NY: Oxford University Press.

Swan, J. A. (1999). *The sacred art of hunting: myths, legends and the modern mythos.* Minocqua,WI: Willow Creek Press.

Tudge, C. (1998). *Neanderthals, bandits and farmers: how agriculture really began.* New Haven, CT: Yale University Press.

Vasey D. E. (1992). *An ecological history of agriculture: 10,000 BC – AD 10,000.* Ames, IA: Iowa State University Press.

Wells, S. (2010). *Pandora's seed: the unforeseen cost of civilization.* New York, NY: Random House.

Wolff, R. (2001). *Original Wisdom: Stories of an Ancient Way of Knowing.* Vermont: Inner Traditions.

Made in the USA
Lexington, KY
30 September 2012